Presented To:

_____

From:

_____

Date:

_____

FASTING
&
PRAYER

DESTINY IMAGE BOOKS BY STEVEN BROOKS

Working With Angels

Standing on the Shoulders of Giants

The Sacred Anointing

FASTING & PRAYER

GOD'S
Nuclear
Power

STEVEN BROOKS

DESTINY IMAGE® PUBLISHERS, INC.
P.O. Box 310, Shippensburg, PA 17257-0310

"Promoting Inspired Lives."

This book and all other Destiny Image, Revival Press, MercyPlace, Fresh Bread, Destiny Image Fiction, and Treasure House books are available at Christian bookstores and distributors worldwide.

For a U.S. bookstore nearest you, call 1-800-722-6774.
For more information on foreign distributors, call 717-532-3040.
Reach us on the Internet: www.destinyimage.com.

ISBN 13 TP: 978-0-7684-4115-4
ISBN 13 Ebook: 978-0-7684-8816-6

For Worldwide Distribution, Printed in the U.S.A.

1 2 3 4 5 6 7 8 / 16 15 14 13 12

DEDICATION

    This book would not be possible without the constant love and support from my dear wife Kelly. As we have traveled the world together she has always been willing to sacrifice in every way to see the work of the Lord go forward. Many of the miracles that have happened in this ministry would not have occurred if it were not for the countless hours she has worked behind the scenes to assist in making it all possible. My marriage and family life have brought me much joy and happiness and it only continues to increase. The Lord has poured out His rich blessing upon my life, and in many ways I feel overwhelmed by His goodness. With a grateful heart I dedicate this book to my wife and my children, for I have seen that the words of the psalmist are true.

Blessed is every one who fears the Lord, who walks in His ways. When you eat the labor of your hands, you shall be happy, and it shall be well with you. Your wife shall be like a fruitful vine in the very heart of your house, your children like olive plants all around your table. Behold, thus shall the man be blessed who fears the Lord. The Lord bless you out of Zion, and may you see the good of Jerusalem all the days of your life. Yes, may you see your children's children. Peace be upon Israel! (Psalms 128)

May the Lord give you increase more and more, you and your children. May you be blessed by the Lord, who made heaven and earth (Psalms 115:14-15).

Acknowledgments

Over the years I have read quite a few books on the subject of fasting and prayer. Each and every author contributed special insights that I learned something from. I would like to especially acknowledge Franklin Hall for his writings on this theme. Much of the prayer surge that ushered in the Healing Revival of the late '40s and throughout the '50s was inspired by Brother Hall's teachings on fasting and prayer. There is another Healing Revival that is on the way which will dwarf the previous move from the '40s and '50s. Even though the coming revival has been prophesied by countless men and women of God, it will still not just randomly happen. It has to be prayed down. To receive the fulfillment of these divinely inspired prophecies we must be willing to petition God to release His glory in our midst. Throughout history we have seen the hand of God moved by those who were willing to labor in prayer coupled with fasting. God has not changed; we must reach out to Him with sincere and determined effort.

Of course there are some things you can't learn from reading books. Active participation is the only true school of learning for the subject of fasting and prayer. This is why many of the things I teach in this book are truths I learned over the years by simply going into the prayer closet and pushing back the plate. These are experiences I wish to share with you to inspire you to also fast and pray and see the miraculous hand of God move in your life.

Holy men and women of God from previous generations have also given us shining examples of the amazing results performed by God for those who fasted and prayed. Along with Brother Hall I would like to acknowledge John "Praying" Hyde, Evan Roberts, Charles Finney, Father Nash, William Seymour, Frank Bartleman, and the "unknown" saints around the world who selflessly pursued the Kingdom of God first and set their minds on things above, not on things on the earth.

CONTENTS

PROGRESSING FROM ATOMIC POWER TO NUCLEAR POWER

THE APOSTLE PAUL SAID THAT the spiritual did not come first, but the natural, and after that the spiritual. This is a general principle illustrated often throughout human history, which is that the lower life (the natural world) reveals to us the higher dimension of the spiritual world (see 1 Cor. 15:46).

I would like to share a few insights about nuclear energy before we delve into the study of fasting and prayer. The parallels between nuclear energy and the power gained through fasting and prayer are very similar. Nuclear energy is a form of natural power being utilized in the earth. Fasting and prayer is a form of spiritual power that is boundless in supply because it is connected with God and His infinite resources. By taking a brief look at the history of nuclear power, we can better understand the power of God that is released when we fast and pray.

Scientists are still learning new ways in which nuclear energy can be more safely contained and more highly utilized in releasing its power to meet the energy needs of a growing world population. The Church is also a spiritual Research and Development Lab that God has placed within the earth to unravel the spiritual laws that exist around us.

When we fast and pray, we tap into the very power of God that He has made available for us. The power of God is here for us to use. We need to know as much about it as possible so that we may personally benefit from it, along with using its power to strengthen the Church. This power is also here to aid in bringing the lost souls to salvation in Jesus. There is still power available to heal the sick, to open blind eyes, to see the dead raised, and to cast out evil spirits. There is power for mighty signs and wonders to be performed. With this in mind, let's look briefly at the natural example of nuclear power which God has placed within the earth, and then we will look at an even greater power that every believer has access to through fasting and prayer—the power of God.

From the Beginning

In the 1940s and the early 50s, atomic power was discovered. Today, there is a greater power that scientists have now unlocked, which is nuclear power. Our most advanced submarines and aircraft carriers are all run by nuclear power. Let me give you an example of modern-day nuclear power.

A large aircraft carrier is like a small city. It has over 5,000 men and women who live and work on board. Each day these people must be fed and must take showers as they work in cramped conditions aboard a ship that is longer than three football fields put together. These great ships, despite their massive size and weight of up to 200 million pounds, can cruise at speeds over 40 miles per hour. To move a ship of this gigantic stature through the water at such amazing speed requires tremendous power. Along with all the men and women on board, there are also enormous quantities of food and other supplies to sustain the ship's crew. Enormous amounts of jet fuel must also be stored onboard to fuel the jets, helicopters, and other military vehicles that the ship transports. What is the source of power that moves the ship through the water and supplies the power needed to run a self-contained city of 5,000 people? The answer lies deep within the ship in a well-guarded area that only few have access to. This area is where the nuclear reactor lies.

The nuclear reactor needs a special type of fuel to create this amazing power. The special element needed is called enriched uranium. Working with this material requires the utmost caution and care. This nuclear material is so powerful that propelling the aircraft carrier through the water and meeting all of its other energy needs is all accomplished through one pound of uranium that is the size of a golf ball! This is the equivalent of being able to have on hand continually one million gallons of gasoline. Nuclear power can be stored in a very small package. To store that amount of gasoline would require a large chamber that would be equivalent to a 15 story building. Did you ever stop to think that something so small, only the size of a golf ball, could power such a huge operation? As a result of the use of nuclear power, these special ships are capable of operating for over 20 years without refueling and are expected to have a service life of over 50 years.

We are living in a critical juncture of time when the Lord is now looking down from Heaven and desiring to pour out His power, His glory, and mighty manifestations of His Spirit like we have never seen before. The power of the Holy Spirit is similar to nuclear power. God always has natural examples in the earth to demonstrate spiritual truths. Scientists are now beginning to unravel the secrets of nuclear power to a greater degree. There is still much to learn about nuclear power before we realize its full potential. In the foreseeable future our cars, homes, and many other devices will be powered through nuclear fission. Today we must learn to operate in the nuclear power of God. The nuclear power of God is available to the believer through prayer and fasting.

The reason the church does not see greater manifestations of God's power is because of a failure to fast and pray. If you want to have true power with God and see miracles like we see in the Bible which the great saints of old experienced, then we must also take up the mantle of fasting and prayer. The desperate needs of our end-time generation cannot be met any other way. The faith that moves mountains, raises the dead, opens blind eyes, heals the sick, and obtains results that are otherwise out of reach are found through the release of God's nuclear power—fasting and prayer.

God is unlocking the secrets of clean nuclear power to scientists so that our future may be cleaner and energy requirements around the world will be better met. As of 2011, there are well over 400 nuclear reactors in the world with another 60 already under construction. In France, 77 percent of the country's electricity comes from nuclear power. America has the most nuclear power plants which supply 20 percent of its energy, with some states benefitting more than others.[1] With growing energy usage in the fields of space, medicine, military, and aviation it's clear that nuclear power is here to stay.

To understand how powerful fasting and prayer can be, let's look at a few examples from the natural realm and see what nuclear energy can produce when released through a nuclear weapon. The explosive yield of a nuclear weapon is measured in kilotons. A kiloton is the explosive force of one thousand tons of TNT. On August 6, 1945, America's Air Force dropped an atomic bomb called Little Boy on Hiroshima, Japan. The bomb exploded with an energy of about 15 kilotons. The second bomb, named Fat Boy, was dropped three days later on the city of Nagasaki with an energy of 21 kilotons. The results were devastating and the Japanese emperor soon surrendered, ending World War II.

Nuclear weapon development continued to progress with America's test detonation of the George, which had an energy of 225 kilotons. In less than two years, America progressed to Ivy Mike, which was equivalent to 10,400 kilotons. In 1954, the United States tested its largest nuclear bomb ever, named Castle Bravo, which produced 15,000 kilotons of energy. Not to be outdone, the Russians in 1961 pulled out all the stops and detonated the largest nuclear weapon of all time, the Tsar Bomba, which produced 57,000 kilotons of energy. The subsequent mushroom cloud was 40 miles high and 25 miles wide. The Tsar Bomba was equivalent to ten times the amount of all the explosives used in World War II combined! It was 4,000 times bigger than the Hiroshima bomb. The massive crater left from the explosion is still visible today from satellite.[2]

The nuclear arms buildup known as the Cold War was responsible for the erecting of the Berlin Wall in Germany. This was a sinful consequence caused by ungodly men who perverted the potential good use of nuclear power into acts of destruction combined with intimidating propaganda. Known as the Iron Curtain, the Berlin Wall was built to keep Eastern and Western Europe separated. For 28 years Germany was divided. The Berlin Wall was regarded around the world as a major symbol of communist oppression. Yet in 1989 the impossible happened; the wall came down. The famous words of President Ronald Reagan, "Mr. Gorbachev, tear down this wall!" were spoken in 1987.[3] I've stood where the wall was once erected. Most of it has been removed now, but I have a small piece of the wall with the metal rebar running through it that was given to me as a gift by a high-ranking German police sergeant. When I go to Berlin to minister, I always like to see where the wall once stood. It blesses me to see how evil was overcome by good. Many pastors and godly men and women prayed and fasted for the wall to come down, and God heard and answered their cries in a miraculous way.

One pastor, whose church I have ministered in several times in Berlin, told me how he and many other German pastors fasted and prayed for 40 days with no food as they petitioned for God to bring down the wall. God even told my friend when the wall was going to fall! He prophesied what the Lord had told him; people were shocked when it happened, but he and the others who fasted and prayed knew it was coming. When his prophecy came to pass he was featured in several of the nation's largest magazines, which was a testimony to his faith in Jesus as well as validating the continued importance of the gift of prophecy. Nothing is impossible with God. When we seek Him with fasting and prayer there is no limit as to what God can do.

There is a lot of misinformation in the church regarding fasting and prayer. We see this mirrored in the world regarding a fear and misunderstanding of nuclear power. In 2011, Japan experienced a powerful earthquake followed immediately by a rushing tsunami. Due to the devastating effects of these consecutive disasters, the backup systems for the nuclear power plants failed. The tsunami swept over the retaining walls and submerged the backup generators that were supposed to power the facilities in case of a loss of power. If the generators had been placed at a higher elevation they would have been able to do their job as planned. The flaw of having the generators at too low of an elevation contributed to the explosions and partial nuclear meltdowns that later occurred. Without electrical power, the nuclear plants could not be properly cooled. The nuclear meltdowns only added to the sorrow caused by the earthquake and tsunami.

The nuclear plant at Fukushima was an old and outdated plant built with cost cutting measures and inadequate safety features that should have been retired years earlier. The new plants that are being constructed today have multiple backup redundant systems that have an extremely high level of safety. Some of the new reactors being made in China have the ability to cool themselves in case of an emergency. Despite the concerns of many about nuclear energy, it is without doubt that nuclear power is here to stay. China and India are leading the world in the building of new nuclear plants. The population of these two countries is growing at such an explosive rate that the use of oil and the pollutants caused by it gives them confidence in choosing nuclear power. If you have ever visited China or India you see immediately the dilemma they are faced with. Large cities are crowded with millions upon millions of people. The need for electricity is enormous. The pollution in the air is mind-boggling. One of the worst cases of air pollution that I have personally witnessed is Calcutta, India. The sky is dark and dirty with the thick and toxic pollution caused by countless rickshaws that spew fumes into the air on a nonstop basis.

China is just as bad when it comes to creating dirty air. This proved to be a real embarrassment to China during the Summer Olympics which were hosted in Beijing in 2008. Some world-class runners were refusing to compete in the marathon because of the potential health hazards of breathing the toxic air for prolonged periods of time. Eventually Chinese authorities got the city's pollution problem under control to ensure their political propaganda machine came across (at least temporarily) as reflecting China in a good light for the Olympic Games. Once the games were over it was back to normal with creating high levels of pollution through the use of oil-based fuels.

There are really only two primary choices for fuel—either oil or nuclear. Solar and wind technologies are still years away from being productive because they can't be commercialized on a large scale to power large cities. Solar and wind technologies rely on natural phenomena that aren't available all the time, but nuclear power plants deliver large amounts of power for long periods of time. Oil and natural gas will always be around because they are naturally replenished from the earth's core. Oil is not a fossil fuel—it does not come from decayed plant matter and decomposed dinosaurs. Despite what some scientists say, oil is a product that is naturally replenished, and God created the earth in a way that there will always be a supply of oil that rises from the earth's core and becomes trapped in reservoirs for future use. (Please see the endnotes for further understanding of where oil comes from and other common myths associated with oil.)[4]

Oil is messy, creates environmental pollution, and is costly to convert to a usable product. Besides, it is good to have diversity in our energy sources. Putting the majority of our demand upon oil to meet our energy needs is not wise, especially when our primary oil supply comes from foreign countries who often do not share our interests or values. When a country produces its own nuclear power, it produces energy security. Oil prices can be hiked up by foreign countries, causing unscrupulous prices people must pay to fuel their vehicles, or through diplomatic crisis oil supply can be cut off entirely. When a country or state uses nuclear energy, no foreign entity can control it. Nuclear energy is part of the equation to help provide ever-increasing global energy needs. Nuclear power is here to stay.

Recently I talked in-depth to a physics professor regarding future energy ideas that are on the horizon. In the physics community there is much discussion about controlling nuclear fission to a degree that it can power almost anything, even our cars. But I was told this technology is still about 100 years away. Perhaps this can be sped up with the new knowledge and understanding that the Lord Jesus will release into the earth.

But you, Daniel, shut up the words, and seal the book until the time of the end; many shall run to and fro, **and knowledge shall increase** (Daniel 12:4).

Although nuclear power has been largely misunderstood in the past, today more and more people are coming to realize its benefits. Fasting has also been a subject that has not been revealed in its true light. Often viewed as an extreme or fanatical practice, it is now being discovered in the light of its natural healing and spiritual benefits when combined with prayer. In the past, nuclear power and fasting have both been painted with a negative tone due to isolated incidents that were not a true reflection of their great value.

We have now seen the natural power available through nuclear energy and nuclear weapons, and we have looked briefly at the future role of nuclear plants in alleviating growing energy needs. As nuclear energy is produced through a nuclear reactor, so God desires for His power to be displayed through us. Would you like to become a nuclear power plant for God? Do you desire to be filled with the power of God and work miracles even as Jesus did? Would you like to see your church become a spiritual version of a fully operational nuclear reactor that is able to meet the desperate needs of your community?

If so, then this book will help you unleash the mighty ability of God in a sustained, clean, and powerful way just like the most advanced nuclear plants do. Let no distraction keep you from leaning into these biblical truths. You do not need to hold a theological degree and you are not required to read biblical Hebrew and Greek. If you do possess these skills then that is wonderful, but God can still work through you even if you are only a child. All the Lord needs is your humble response and simple obedience. Embrace what the Word of God teaches concerning fasting combined with fervent prayer, be a hearer and a doer of the Word of God, and the power of God will flow through you to see even the most impossible prayers answered and countless other needs and desires met.

Endnotes

1. "How Nuclear Power Works," HowStuffWorks, accessed September 27, 2011, http://science.howstuffworks.com/nuclear-power.htm; and "Nuclear Power Plants Worldwide," European Nuclear Society, accessed September 27, 2011, http://www.euronuclear.org/info/encyclopedia/n/nuclear-power-plant-world-wide.htm.

2. "Tsar Bomba," Wikipedia, the Free Encyclopedia, accessed September 27, 2011, http://en.wikipedia.org/wiki/Tsar_Bomba.

3. "Berlin Wall," Wikipedia, the Free Encyclopedia, accessed September 27, 2011, http://en.wikipedia.org/wiki/Berlin_Wall.

4. Jerome R. Corsi and Craig R. Smith, *Black Gold Stranglehold: The Myth of Scarcity and the Politics of Oil* (Nashville, TN: WND Books, 2005).

Chapter One

Divine Radiation

Moses was on the mountain of Sinai in the presence of God for 40 days. While he was there he received the Ten Commandments along with other important information regarding laws, regulations, and the plans for the earthly tabernacle. Upon his descent from the mountain, he found the people unrestrained, committing fornication, and a total absence of leadership. In his righteous anger, he broke the two tablets of stone upon which were written the Ten Commandments. After some very necessary days of putting things back in order, he was again summoned by God to go up the mountain for another extended meeting. This second trip to the summit of Mount Sinai lasted again for 40 days. In the presence of the Lord, we see that Moses had no natural appetite or thirst.

So he was there with the Lord forty days and forty nights; he neither ate bread nor drank water. And He wrote on the tablets the words of the covenant, the Ten Commandments (Exodus 34:28).

While in the Lord's presence Moses did not eat or drink for 40 days. Some people describe this as a supernatural fast, but the Bible does not identify this as a fast. If you and I were translated to Heaven for 40 days and we stayed there for the entire time, we would not require food or water. In Heaven you can eat if you want to, but you don't have to because you don't experience hunger or thirst like here on earth. You may eat for fun or for the joy of taste, but it is not necessary for strength or energy. So Moses was not on a fast. Yet we still see a wonderful example of the benefits of being away from the natural world for an extended period of time. This is essentially what takes place when we do fast from food. We come into a heightened awareness of the realm of God's Spirit and we are able to receive "downloads" of heavenly information that God desires to impart to us.

When Moses came down from the mountain, he was not aware that the skin on his face was glowing. As he tried to talk to Aaron and others, they were afraid of him. Moses decided to put a veil over his face so they would feel comfortable around him. He was radiating the glory of God.

When Jesus experienced the transfiguration on the mountain at night, He had with Him Peter, James, and John. While the three disciples slept, the Lord was transfigured and His true glory blazed outward with great brilliance. The Gospel narratives do not tell you what caused the three disciples to wake up, but I believe I know what woke them up. Have you ever been sound asleep in a dark room and in a comfortable bed, and someone comes in the middle of the night and unexpectedly turns the lights fully on? Well, instantly you would wake up. The glory emanating from Jesus woke Peter, James, and John up from their deep sleep. Peter probably rolled over and said, "Hey John, I can't believe the sun is coming up already!" It is the glory of God, and nothing but the brilliant glory of God that is going to awaken the sleeping Church and get her up on her feet!

Jesus spoke with Moses and Elijah while on the mountain. The next morning as He came down with the three disciples, the crowd met Him with an unusual reaction.

> *And when He came to the disciples, He saw a great multitude around them, and scribes disputing with them. Immediately, when they saw Him, all the people were greatly amazed, and running to Him, greeted Him* (Mark 9:14-15).

For some time, I was puzzled by the phrase *"all the people were greatly amazed."* It was still early in the morning and Jesus had not even ministered yet that day. All He did was walk toward the people. But what had happened to Him was the same thing that happened to Moses. The divine radiance of God was beaming through Him. The people saw it and were amazed. Many of the old paintings done of Jesus often have a halo pictured over Him. This was an attempt by the artists to express the glory that at certain times was visibly seen upon Jesus.

Our mountaintop experiences are for the purpose of filling us up so that we can minister to the needs of those at the bottom of the mountain. Jesus walked off the mountain right into the middle of a mess. The other nine disciples were not able to cast a demon out of a boy. Jesus took charge of the situation and cast the demon out with no problem. The disciples asked Jesus privately why they could not do it.

> *So He said to them, "This kind can come out by nothing but prayer and fasting"* (Mark 9:29).

If you want to walk in a realm where the radioactive nuclear power of God flows out of you, then you must pray and fast.

Wouldn't it be easy on our fleshly nature if Jesus would instead have said, "This kind can come out by nothing but playing and feasting"? If that were the case then the Church today would be mighty in deliverance power. But we can't change a single word of God. There are no shortcuts to the true power Source.

> In the model Church, the people will love to pray. They will love that more than anything else. They would rather go to a prayer meeting than to a place of entertainment. When the Church of God uses the Apostolic standard, it will be a praying church; that will be its chief characteristic. —Gipsy Smith

One of my favorite examples in the Bible is the one of Peter when he has tapped fully into the power of God. Because we have an outstanding example demonstrated by Peter, it should forever settle the question of, "Can we walk in this same level of power?"

*And believers were increasingly added to the Lord, multitudes of both men and women, so that they brought the sick out into the streets and laid them on beds and couches, **that at least the shadow of Peter passing by might fall on some of them.** Also a multitude gathered from the surrounding cities to Jerusalem, bringing sick people and those who were tormented by unclean spirits, **and they were all healed** (Acts 5:14-16).*

Peter was a normal man just like anybody else. Having been with Jesus for His entire three years of ministry, he saw first-hand the power of God demonstrated. Later, after the Lord's ascension into Heaven, Peter was mightily filled with the immersion of the Holy Spirit as recorded in Acts 2. The anointing on his life increased to the degree that on certain occasions a person within the proximity of his shadow was healed. That's a strong anointing. One way you could grasp this is by thinking of Peter as being radioactive. He was emitting something. Without question, something powerful was coming off of him. If it were possible for Peter to walk in this anointing, then it is possible for you to experience this as well. Peter had learned through the Lord's teaching the great truths of prayer and fasting. This was meat and potatoes for all of the twelve apostles and the early church leaders.

The divine radiation of God destroys sickness, disease, depression, yokes, bondages, and drives out demon spirits. The nuclear power of God is beyond anything the enemy can produce. Demons are terrified of an anointed man, woman, or young person who has their nuclear reactor in full production.

Many years ago I made a mistake when I was leading a meeting. I was the chapter president of a Christian businessmen's luncheon. Each week my wife and I would invite a successful businessman or businesswoman to come and share their testimony. Each week people were saved, healed, or filled with the Spirit or experienced all three at the same time! One week, the scheduled speaker unexpectedly did not arrive. Just before starting the meeting he called me and expressed his regret that he would not be able to make it on time due to an unexpected delay. So, I was left sitting there wondering what to do for a speaker. Then, unexpectedly, a minister friend of mine walked into the room to join our luncheon. It had been quite some time since I last saw him, but it was a pleasant surprise for him to drop in. The thing that was amazing to Kelly and I was that when he walked into the room there was a wonderful soft and glowing light radiating from his face. He looked like an angel.

When I saw my minister friend I asked him to come and sit next to me at the head table. Leaning over to him as we ate, I asked him, "Did you know your face is illuminated? What have you been doing?"

He replied, "I just finished fasting for three days with no food and just water to drink. During the three days I was in prayer."

Since my scheduled speaker was unable to come I asked all of the people there to just have a time of Christian fellowship together as we all enjoyed a great meal. My big mistake was not asking my friend to speak and minister to the people. But we learn as we go, and I catch on real quick and have tried to stay alert to not miss other divine opportunities.

There have been many times when I have seen other believers walking in a physically visible manifestation of glory. When it covers a person, it looks like one is enshrouded with light. When you read about Adam and Eve in the Garden of Eden, it appears they were also covered with this same divine light. Here is how they are described before they sinned:

And they were both naked, the man and his wife, and were not ashamed (Genesis 2:25).

And here is how they are described after they sinned:

Then the eyes of both of them were opened, and they knew that they were naked; and they sewed fig leaves together and made themselves coverings (Genesis 3:7).

Sin is a natural blocker of the glory of God. Adam and Eve were originally clothed with the glory of God but lost this covering upon committing sin. Jesus has restored us back to God the

Father so that we can again walk in this blessed state. We can radiate the glory of God just as Peter did. Sick people were being healed without even having hands laid on them for prayer. Just getting within shadow-proximity of Peter when he was operating in a strong anointing, resulted in healing. This also happens in my own healing ministry. The following testimony shares one such case.

> Hi Steven, I was on the 2010 tour with you to Israel. You had prayed for my legs and ankles. Well, a couple of days later I was in pain and my ankles were swollen and painful again. I was going to ask you for prayer again but so many people were coming to you, I didn't want to bother you. So I slowly crept closer toward you but again I stopped not wanting to bother you. I crept closer again and was just a foot away and I decided to not bother you, when I felt a warmth go through my ankles and the pain left. I couldn't believe it. God healed me by just standing next to you. Thank you, Father God and thank you, Steven. I just wanted you to know the anointing power of God that is on and all around you without you doing anything. Thank you, Sylvia D.

This divine radiation is increasing upon us individually and also as a church body. The length of Peter's shadow will be extended. Churches that are devoted to lifestyles of prayer and fasting will see the salvation and healing glory extend to cover entire city blocks. Churches outside of cities in rural areas will see the glory cover large expanses of land. Large crowds numbering into the hundreds of thousands will gather in remote areas. People will go to where the power is being manifested; it's a simple truth demonstrated time and time again.

As we become carriers of His glory, we fulfill the Old Testament example of the Ark of the Covenant. In the tabernacle of

Moses and the Temple of Solomon, the Ark of the Covenant was the most sacred item of all and kept in the most sacred place, inside the Most Holy Place behind a thick veiled curtain. Only once a year was the high priest allowed to go behind the curtain to offer atonement for the sins of the people. The annual act was very solemn and done in fear and trepidation. The High Priest was the only person who ever saw the Ark of the Covenant. The general community of believing Jews had no direct access to God.

Today we have a much different scenario. When Jesus shed His blood for us at Calvary, He acted as High Priest on our behalf. Upon His death, the veil in the temple was torn from the top to the bottom (see Matt. 27:51). For the first time, the inside of the Most Holy Place could be seen. Jesus made access to the Father for us. There is no longer any separation. Not only can we come before God, but we can actually come boldly before the throne of grace with a clear and clean conscience (see Heb. 4:16). Now, because Jesus lives in you, you are an ark for His glory. This was a concept that very few of the Old Testament saints understood.

David was a man who did grasp the future realities that the Messiah Jesus would one day fulfill. This is why David ate the showbread and was not struck dead by God (see 1 Sam. 21:4-6). David knew that the showbread and other pieces of furniture were meant to represent heavenly realities. He understood these items were meant to convey symbolic truths that spoke of a coming Messiah. This is also why David and Bathsheba were not stoned to death, even though they committed adultery and the law required them to be stoned. David understood the concept of grace and knew that the Old Testament tabernacle, the items used in the tabernacle, feast days, dietary laws, and many other laws and regulations were *"a shadow of things to come, but the substance is of Christ"* (Col. 2:17).

When we fast and pray, the glory of God will radiate outward from within our hearts. We then become an ark that God lives in and displays Himself through.

Once I was in Hamburg, Germany to conduct the wedding of my oldest daughter, Jennifer. She is now married to Alex, a fine gentleman of German descent. While in Hamburg preparing for the wedding, we had to go to the rehearsal to make sure everything went smoothly for the big day. For several days I had been seeking God with fasting and prayer for His anointing to rest upon me for upcoming meetings that I would later conduct while in Germany. I was traveling with the father of my son-in-law. The German father of the groom drove a nice big Mercedes Benz. He was a strong, traditional German, but he and I couldn't communicate because he didn't speak any English and I couldn't speak any German.

We were driving along enjoying a beautiful day on the way to the church building. I was sitting in the front passenger seat and my youngest daughter, Abigail, was riding in the back seat behind me. As we drove smoothly along we came to an intersection but we did not have to stop, just the other connecting streets did. Suddenly a car coming from another direction ran through its stop sign. The other driver not only ran through his stop sign but he also never even slowed down. He was speeding and coming at us from a rear-side angle in what appeared to be an unavoidable collision. We all braced for impact. The reckless driver and his car swerved directly into us.

Time slowed down and everything appeared to go into slow motion. His car merged right into our car but there was no impact. His car passed three feet inside of our car and passed through me and Abigail. A miracle occurred as both cars continued traveling forward while passing through each other. Then suddenly we separated as the other car swerved off on another exit street and drove speedily away. Alex's father never said a word to me, but he looked as white as a sheet and was sweating profusely. He was a staunch Lutheran and had never experienced anything like that before.

The next day Alex told me that his father described to his family what took place. Alex said after the near accident that his father was shaking uncontrollably for the remainder of the day. He had never been in a life-threatening situation like that before. The father was stunned when with his own eyes he saw the two cars blend together as one and drive together before separating without any collision or damage. He told his son Alex, "Truly, the man I was traveling with is a holy man of God."

When we radiate the glory of Jesus, others see it and consider its value. Often our best messages are not what we preach or say, but how God shines through us. As you fast and pray, you position yourself to be clothed with the glory of God to emit His divine radiation to bring salvation and healing to others.

A lifestyle of prayer and fasting will also create a shield of divine protection around you that the enemy cannot penetrate. There have been countless times when the enemy has tried to take my life, but God always supplied His protection. When you are on the front lines ministering the Gospel and delivering people out of the kingdom of darkness, the enemy doesn't take that lightly. The great evangelist Charles Finney was also aware of such tactics of the devil, as he shares in the following story.

Accordingly the next Sunday after preaching the second time, one of the new converts offered to take me up to Stephentown in his carriage. When he came to me I asked him, "Have you a steady horse?"

"Oh, yes!" he replied, "perfectly so," and smiling, he asked, "What made you ask the question?"

"Because," I replied, "if the Lord wants me to go to Stephentown the devil will prevent it if he can, and if you do not have a steady horse, he will try to make him kill me."

He smiled and we rode on. Strange to tell, before we got there that horse ran away twice and came near killing us. His owner expressed the greatest astonishment and said he had never known such a thing before.[1]

When you walk in the nuclear power of God, you are a great threat to the devil and his kingdom. The devil will throw all types of road blocks and difficulties in your path, but through Christ we are more than conquerors. If you want to radiate the divine power of God and demonstrate His miracle-working power, it is important for you to realize that persecutions, discouragement, and resistance will come your way. You must resolve now to not let this deter you from walking in love and staying on the course God has for you.

Once, I was invited to go preach a meeting in Pennsylvania. While talking on the phone with the pastor, he told me that he had a church of 300 people and that if I would come, we would have a great meeting. I agreed to come and arrived the day before the meeting, so I would not have to rush. He insisted I stay at an apartment room next to the church, which he said was fully furnished and owned by the church. He gave me the key and he drove away to take care of some other business he had. I walked up some outside stairs to go inside the apartment and couldn't help but notice the stairs appeared to be barely able to support my weight without collapsing. I asked Kelly not to come up the stairs for fear they might fall down.

As I opened the door to the apartment, I was overwhelmed with the smell of mold and mildew. As my eyes adjusted to the apartment's dim light I noticed green mold on the walls and old, worn-out beige carpet dating back to the early 1970s. The carpet appeared to be wet and all the furnishings reeked with smoke. The place was very dirty. Just out of curiosity, I decided to check the refrigerator to see if the pastor left with me with any food. Before driving away, he said the apartment was fully furnished, including food. Upon opening the fridge, I saw one loaf of bread that had molded so badly that one half of the loaf was green and the other a dark yellow color. To complete the bountiful provision that he had left for me, there was one jar of mustard and a bottle of water to feast on. I walked back down the stairs and saw Kelly. She said, "What was that awful smell coming from out of there?"

I replied, "Excuse me, dear, while I make a little phone call to the pastor."

I called the pastor and informed him of the smoke and mildew. He said, "Oh, we had a fire a few months back and then our hot water heater exploded. We haven't been able to do any cleaning yet. I was kinda wondering myself what those foul smells were."

"Well, I can't stay in there," I said. "That place is not suitable for humans to live in. The dangerous fumes would make a person sick."

There was a slow pause, and then with a slight hesitation he said, "OK, let me put you in a hotel instead."

I checked into the hotel and prepared myself for the evening meeting. When it came time for the service to start that night, there were only eight people in the meeting. I asked the pastor, "Where are the people? You said over the phone just three weeks ago that you had three hundred members!"

"Well, we had a little falling-out recently, but more will come in as the service progresses."

"What about advertising for the meeting?" I asked him. "Did you do any?"

Shrugging his shoulders he said, "That sort of slipped by us. I meant to call the people but ran out of time." The service soon began and there was a time of praise and worship and then it was time for me to minister. The size of the crowd had now swelled to 15 people. Thoughts floated through my mind suggesting, "You spent all that time in prayer and fasting for nothing. This meeting is going to be a real flop." But inwardly I prayed and said, "Heavenly Father, I'm going to minister this evening to these 15 people as if I were preaching to 15,000. Let your Spirit flow."

That evening I preached the Word to that small group, and I could sense the presence of the Lord draw near. Everyone present in the meeting was already saved, but four ladies from another city had seen my travel schedule on the internet and had come to hear me preach. They also brought a lady to the meeting in need of prayer. After ministering the Word, I asked those to come forward who would like prayer. The four ladies came up front and one of them said, "We came here tonight to ask you to pray for our friend. She has just become a Christian, but she needs deliverance from the devil who still torments her."

The woman who needed prayer was an African-American woman in her mid-forties. She had just been saved, but I could see the devil still had a stronghold over her life. The Holy Spirit spoke to me and said, "She is under the power of a Muslim spirit."

Reaching my hand out, I gently touched this woman on the forehead with just one finger. When I did, she screamed and fell to the floor and lay there in a heap. She stayed on the floor for about one minute, then as she began to stand she started speaking in tongues for the very first time. She was so under the influence of the Holy Spirit that she also began to prophesy, declaring the glory and wonder of God. The meeting ended shortly thereafter because it didn't take very long to pray for fifteen people.

The next night I was ministering in a different church in a different town about an hour away. The same four ladies came to that meeting also and they brought their friend back. The lady who was prayed for shared a beautiful testimony. She told us that when I touched her with my finger, a bolt of lightning shot through her from above. As she lay on the floor the Lord Jesus walked up to her in a vision and confirmed her salvation, and then He baptized her in His Holy Spirit. She stood up filled with the Spirit and forever set free from her former Muslim darkness.

Now this lady was in her mid-forties in age, but when she woke up that morning and walked outside of her house, for the first time in her life she noticed that the sky was blue! All her life from a child to a grown adult as a Muslim, she thought the sky was gray. When seeing that the sky was actually a beautiful blue, she was overwhelmed with love and appreciation to the Lord Jesus.

Upon returning home, Kelly and I ran into a friend who used to live in Iran but now has immigrated to America, and we shared with him about this woman's conversion. He said, "Yes, when a Muslim is truly converted, they often see Jesus and the 'gray scale' comes off their eyes when they are filled with the Spirit. This is a common occurrence that is taking place in the Arab world."

So, despite the tough going and shameful treatment from that pastor, I am eternally glad I chose to pray and fast so that I could minister in the anointing. Even if only one person's life was touched, I am thankful beyond words. We must endure and reflect the "divine radiation" of Jesus even in the midst of trials and difficulties.

Ministry brings much joy, but the work of the ministry can at times be very demanding. We see this with the disciples who followed Jesus and helped in many ways during the large miracle crusades. Often, believers fail to picture what it must have been like during the Lord's earthly ministry. Because of the mighty healing anointing upon His life, there were often great multitudes who flocked to hear Him preach and to receive healing. This placed a great strain upon the twelve disciples as the meetings were jam-packed with people. The disciples assisted with organization and administration, along with many other tasks that are necessary to keep a large ministry running smoothly. At times it appears the demands of ministry seemed to almost overwhelm the small staff of twelve disciples. The following verse gives us a brief glimpse of how hectic the ministry of Jesus could sometimes be.

And He said to them, "Come aside by yourselves to a deserted place and rest a while." For there were many coming and going, **and they did not even have time to eat.** *So they departed to a deserted place in the boat by themselves* (Mark 6:31-32).

The disciples were so busy that sometimes they could not even take a break to eat. The ministry involves sacrifice, but the Lord takes good care of His workers and makes sure to also schedule in times of rest and rejuvenation.

I would rather teach one man to pray than ten men to preach. —Charles Spurgeon

Some time back, I was ministering in a miracle conference in India. This meeting in India was my last meeting before flying

home to North Carolina. I had started my trip one month earlier and traveled through five countries, sometimes doing five meetings in one day. By the time this trip was completed, I had circumnavigated around the whole world. Toward the end of the trip, my body began to experience the fatigue of constant travel. There was the continuous changes through international time zones, weight loss due to eating foods I wasn't accustomed to, the strain of constant preaching, exhausting times of prayer in hot and humid climates, occasional fasting to enhance the anointing, and other irregularities that left me desiring a nice, quiet place to go and rest for a while.

Finally, I was nearing the end of my trip, but I had one more meeting to clear before I could let up and relax. This meeting in India would conclude my one month of apostolic travel. It was a hot night in South India; we were only about ten miles from the shores of the Indian Ocean, which I personally believe is the most beautiful ocean in the world. It was a Sunday evening. Earlier that day I had preached in the morning service. The people were expecting God to move, and the Lord did not disappoint us. As the Spirit began to move, I finished my preaching and then commenced to personally lay hands on every person in the meeting and anoint them with oil as they passed by me in an organized line. There were just over 2,000 people in the meeting.

Upon completing my time of ministry to the people, it was late at night and I was absolutely exhausted. In my body I reached a level of fatigue that I never felt even in competitive sports. After praying for all of those people, I could also sense the anointing of God's Spirit dissipate. After one full month of non-stop meetings, I had reached my threshold of ministry output. I felt like my experience must have been similar to an Olympic weight lifter who gives his greatest effort to lift the heaviest weight possible. There was nothing else to give; I was completely spent.

Even though I had finished praying for the people, no one left and went home. The glory of the Lord brought such deep joy that everyone wanted to stay in the meeting and just sit in the glory. I handed the microphone back to the pastor and sat down. My clothes were drenched with sweat. As I sat there I could see that the kind pastor was overcome with joy. He was so thrilled in the work that God had performed that evening that he suddenly announced with great enthusiasm, "I want everyone to line up again! The Man of God, Pastor Steven Brooks, is going to pray for all of you again so that you can receive a double blessing." He then handed the microphone back to me as the crowd of several thousand people began to form a huge line toward the stage. Summoning my courage and little remaining strength, I began again to pray for the people. When I got to the fourth person in line, suddenly the whole room began spinning and I almost fell down. It was definitely time for me to stop. I simply took the microphone and handed it to a guest minister who had unexpectedly attended the meeting that night. He and I are close friends. I sat down and drank a Coca-Cola while my friend went to work. (You should always be ready, in season and out of season; you never know when you will get called.)

Even though the work of the ministry has stretched me, I would not trade the experience of it for anything. It's all about presenting the living Jesus to the people of the world and walking in fellowship with God. Some of the most challenging times can also be times when you sense His nearness more acutely. Always radiate the Lord's love and mercy toward others. Spend time in the Lord's presence. Receive His light and get a spiritual "Son tan." Soak in His glory.

While leaving a meeting just the other day, a person shook my hand and thanked me for the word I had preached. When he shook my hand he looked at me and said, "Your hand is burning hot."

"Yes," I replied, "it is the Lord's fiery healing anointing." Without saying a word he reached down and grabbed my hand and put it on his head, as he received a mighty touch from God. Allow God to fill you with His glory. Desire all of the spiritual gifts. Radiate the gifts of the Spirit. *You* are to shine forth the attributes of God. *You* are His ambassador in the earth. *You* represent Jesus to the people. Now, go forth and shine for God.

Endnote

1. Charles G. Finney and Helen Wessel, *The Autobiography of Charles G. Finney* (Minneapolis, MN: Bethany Fellowship, 1977), 138.

CHAPTER TWO

FASTING BY GRACE

THE WORD "FASTING" BRINGS MANY different mental images to people when they hear it. There is often a fear associated with fasting, because many Christians misunderstand it. Almost twenty years ago, I was working for a sprinkler irrigation company. I knew there was a calling upon my life to the full-time ministry, so I wanted to try and walk close with the Lord so that the calling would be developed and realized. While working in the summer, the thought came into my heart to do some fasting. From the natural viewpoint this looked very difficult, because we had just gotten a job that would require extensive manual labor. I and another Christian brother were the ditch diggers so that the sprinkler lines could be laid. This was back-breaking work, and that particular week a temperature record was set in West Texas, with temperatures rising to 117 degrees Fahrenheit and never going below 105 for the whole week.

For five days I ate no food and drank only orange juice. We worked at least eight hours every day and each day I did nothing but dig ditches and shovel dirt. During lunchtime we would all sit on the gates of our pick-up trucks and talk and eat. While the others ate, I would sip on a little bit of orange juice. The guy who dug the ditches with me was a huge man. He could naturally bench press over 400 pounds and was very muscular. His name was Thornton but we all called him Thor because he was so strong, much like the superhero from the comic book series. He was concerned about my health and me not eating. He would say, "Brother Steven, please eat some food; I'm concerned you are going to die!"

But I would respond, "No brother, I'm fine; the Lord is my strength." Each day as we worked there was not a single time when I needed an extra rest or could not keep up. While working I would pray nonstop in tongues, and what began to happen was that my friend couldn't keep up with me! Within a few days the other workers began to notice my superhuman strength.

The boss was a Christian man. After three days, when he saw how hard I was working it inspired him to begin an immediate fast. That morning, he left the job site and went to the grocery store and came back with several gallons of orange juice sitting in the front seat of his truck. He was ready to give it a try.

The searing Texas heat quickly began to rise past 110 degrees and held steady at 117. This day the boss was down in the ditches with us laying the plastic PVC pipe to connect the sprinklers. He was drinking juice while he glued the pipe together. Thor and I were sweating gallons of water as we shoveled thousands of pounds of dirt. We had suntans so dark it looked like we were from Egypt! After five hours of work we realized that our boss had disappeared and that we had not seen him for the last hour. We stopped working and began to look for him. We called his name but there was no answer. Finally, we found him laid out in the front seat of his pickup. He had completely collapsed and passed out from exhaustion. When he recovered enough to talk, the first thing he said was, "Steven, I can't do it, I can't do it." He was referring to fasting, and he was disappointed that he didn't have the same experience of energy and strength that occurred for me. Truly, it was the grace of God which came upon me to fast and allowed me to work with a Samson-type anointing. I believe praying in tongues non-stop while digging in the ditches played a vital role in the Spirit supplying me with a strength that was far beyond my natural ability.

We finished our week of work that lasted Monday through Friday, and on Saturday I ate a small salad at lunchtime to break my fast. I never really had any hunger for food during my week on the job, but now I felt like eating. Some friends of mine were going to a healing service in a neighboring state and asked me to come along. I traveled with them and we arrived just before the meeting started. The meeting was hosted by an international minister who ministered in the healing anointing. Because I had spent the week in fasting and set aside time after work to pray, I had become very sensitive to the Holy Spirit. While sitting there in the meeting, my spiritual eyes suddenly opened and I began seeing into the realm of the Spirit just as easily as seeing with my natural eyes. The Shekinah glory of God could be seen hovering in certain places inside the meeting room. As people fell down because of the glory, I could see how the anointing would flow from the minister and go into the bodies of the sick people, causing many to be healed. It was a long meeting, but the whole time my spiritual eyes continued to see into the glory realm. It was during this trip that the Lord spoke to me and said, "You will also operate in the power of My Spirit."

When we fast and pray, we need to expect the grace of God to come upon our lives. When the Holy Spirit helps you, it makes all the difference in the world. There have been times when I would try to fast, but the timing was wrong and the grace to fast was not there. Even if I would try to push through, I would feel miserable and eventually call the attempt off. Some of these things we learn as we progress in our walk with the Lord. We must learn to rely upon the Holy Spirit to guide us when it comes to this area of fasting and experiencing the grace of God to carry us through. God's grace supplies an underlying joy and deep peace in everything we do. If there is no peace or joy then it is best to reevaluate what we are doing.

Once when I was pastoring my first church in California, I had done some fasting to seek the Lord for an upcoming meeting. Because we were just starting the church, I had a lot of extra tasks to get done, which is difficult when your energy level is low. As the evening church service drew near, I could tell that my energy was almost depleted, so I took a little rest and sat down and waited, as I had about thirty minutes left before the meeting started.

Just before the meeting was to begin, I noticed a large sound speaker not being used that had not been put away in a storage closet. Quickly I went over and picked it up and carried it up some stairs to put it away. As I walked back down the stairs, I realized I had probably overextended myself physically. What little energy I had left had now evaporated from lifting and carrying that heavy object. I started the meeting and then we had a short time of praise and worship before I spoke my message. As I walked to the pulpit to preach I felt very fatigued, but I tried to shake it off and dig deep to carry on. After talking for about ten minutes the room slowly began to spin around. My legs quickly became wobbly, and I collapsed on the carpet in front of the startled church members! A few of the men ushers came and picked me up and laid me out on the front pew of the sanctuary. My head was still spinning and I was disoriented. Kelly was wiping my forehead with a handkerchief and my oldest daughter, Jennifer, was standing next to me.

Although it took great effort to speak, I managed to ask Jennifer for some specific help. My voice could barely be heard so she had to lean her ear very close in order to hear me speak. I said, "Jennifer, back in the church kitchen there is a large glass bottle of grape juice in the refrigerator. Please bring it to me; it will help me to feel better." I knew drinking grape juice would give me an energy boost because it contains natural sugar. While laying there waiting for Jennifer to return, Kelly handed me the wireless microphone. I held it close to my mouth and said with a soft voice, "Due to unforeseen difficulties, tonight's service is cancelled." Even though I said this most of the people stayed around and prayed for me.

Within a minute, Jennifer returned from the kitchen with the large bottle of grape juice. As I took it in my hand I was assisted up into a sitting position there on the pew. I took the lid off the bottle and began to guzzle it down as fast as I could. Suddenly, I realized that something was terribly wrong. I began to cough and spew the grape juice out of my mouth, but it was too late, I had already drunk almost half the bottle. I held the bottle up to my eyes and said, "Hey, wait a minute, this is not our church's grape juice."

The building we were renting also was used by another church. The other church had left an old bottle of grape juice in the refrigerator, and Jennifer unknowingly had grabbed their juice, not ours. Upon looking at the bottom of the bottle, I saw that the juice was bottled nine years earlier. Over the years it had completely fermented into alcohol! The ushers laid me back down on the front row pew and passed me the microphone. I had gone from bad to worse. With a very quiet voice I said, "Due to further unforeseen difficulties, all other remaining services for the week are also cancelled!"

When God's grace is there, things flow smoothly; when it's not, we often don't make it as far as we had hoped. Again, these are things we learn as we progress in our walk with the Lord. I would rather push a little too hard in my quest for spiritual gain than be bound with spiritual lethargy and never make any strides forward.

I have found prayer and fasting the greatest joy, and you will always find it so when you are led by God.
—Smith Wigglesworth

The godly saint from India, Sadhu Sundar Singh, also had a similar experience when he endeavored to do a 40-day fast. In February 1913, he attempted a 40-day fast in a jungle near Rishikesh. After about twenty days of fasting, he passed out and was discovered by bamboo woodcutters. He was carried to a Christian parsonage where he was nursed back to health. I would suspect the reason he passed out was because he was not drinking enough water. Actually, he may not have been drinking any water at all, because he sat down under a tree in the jungle and never moved from there.

He was attempting to do a 40-day fast just like Jesus. But what some believers don't realize is that Jesus drank water during His fast. This is why the devil tempted Him to turn the stones into bread, because Jesus was hungry but He was not thirsty. There were obviously springs or streams that Jesus drank from during His 40-day fast from food. Yet even still, Sundar Singh attributed a notable increase in his spiritual life to his fast, allowing him to gain mastery over impatience and certain doubts. During his fast, he saw a powerful vision of Jesus with pierced hands, bleeding feet, and radiant face. Sadhu confessed that this vision cleared away all of his doubts about living the devoted life of a Christian Sadhu (holy man) and delivered him from all his weaknesses and fears. Those who knew him considered him more like Jesus than anyone else they had ever met.

As we fast in the will of God, there is a grace from God that comes and rests upon us. God's grace is similar to exercise. When you start out on an early morning run, you may initially feel stiff and out of your rhythm. But after running for about ten minutes, you start to loosen up as your body warms up. Now your muscles begin to feel relaxed and loose, and you can enjoy your time of exercise. You know the grace of God is with you when you fast and feel that you are in a comfortable rhythm. For example, there have been people who decide to fast for seven days, but upon reaching that point and feeling fine, they continue on to day 14. Upon reaching this milestone, some still feel fine and continue the fast until the 21-day mark. Some reach this goal and still feel God's grace is with them and they end up doing a 40-day fast, which was never their original intent because it seemed beyond their normal ability. The opposite can happen when we endeavor to fast, but it is not done in the proper time or method.

For instance, God would not have you fast if it were to impede your ability to properly perform your daily work. To not perform your work with diligence and with all your heart would run against God's Word, which clearly directs us to work to the very best of our abilities. It would be an awful Christian witness to perform shoddy work with the excuse that we are tired due to fasting. This is why many people fast using fruit or vegetable juice because it will supply energy to your body so that you can still perform your daily work without being exhausted.

I rely upon the grace of God because I am not an ascetic type of person. An ascetic is by definition someone who inflicts pain and punishment upon themselves and practices extreme self-denial. Asceticism is a deceptive tactic of the enemy and far removed from the biblical practices of prayer and fasting. In the centuries past, some well-intentioned saints would actually whip themselves in an attempt to try to subdue their carnal desires. The devil tries to push people into extremism, but the ways of God are peaceful and gentle.

> *But the wisdom that is from above is first pure, then peaceable, gentle, willing to yield, full of mercy and good fruits, without partiality and without hypocrisy* (James 3:17).

> *Such regulations indeed have an appearance of wisdom, with their self-imposed worship, their false humility and their harsh treatment of the body, but they lack any value in restraining sensual indulgence* (Colossians 2:23 NIV).

God created food to be enjoyed, so when the Holy Spirit leads a child of God to fast, there is a grace that accompanies that desire. Just like anyone else, I enjoy a good meal. From New York-style pizza to classic all-American cheeseburgers to Chilean Sea Bass, it's all good and I always try to save a little room for dessert, such as mouth-watering key lime pie or strawberry cake with butter crème frosting. When fasting by grace, the normal appetite is suspended so that you can be free to focus on prayer and being spiritually perceptive.

While there can be leadings of the Holy Spirit to fast, it is not necessary to have a special leading. You can fast by simply choosing to pursue a closer walk with God. While I don't agree with ascetic practices, I also am not going to sit back and let my fleshly nature run out of control. You don't have to have a special leading to fast and pray. It is normal to crucify the old Adamic nature that tries to usurp Christian conduct. Jesus made this point quite clear.

If your hand causes you to sin, cut it off. It is better for you to enter into life maimed, rather than having two hands, to go to hell, into the fire that shall never be quenched—where "Their worm does not die and the fire is not quenched."

And if your foot causes you to sin, cut it off. It is better for you to enter life lame, rather than having two feet, to be cast into hell, into the fire that shall never be quenched—where "Their worm does not die and the fire is not quenched."

And if your eye causes you to sin, pluck it out. It is better for you to enter the kingdom of God with one eye, rather than having two eyes, to be cast into hell fire—where "Their worm does not die and the fire is not quenched" (Mark 9:43-48).

In these verses, the Lord Jesus does not literally mean we are to go out and gouge our eyes out. Even blind people can have problems of lust the same as those with perfect vision. We do not need to take a saw and cut off our hand or foot, because if we are intent on sinning then we will do it even if we have to acquire robotic assistance. The point that He is strongly trying to emphasize is that we need to deal severely with the carnal nature and shut down ungodly desires.

As the old military proverb says "Loose lips sink ships!" This saying was used during World War II to warn Allied soldiers of unguarded talk that might give useful information to the enemy. Rules of conduct were made, which included subjects that the soldiers were not allowed to publicly talk about.

It is also true today that loose living sinks your spiritual life. When Moses was up on Mount Sinai for 40 days and 40 nights, he was unaware of the activity happening down below in the Israelites camp until he was informed by the Lord to go down and see what was taking place. Aaron failed to lead the people in a godly manner. His desire to be accepted and popular amongst the people was a recipe for disaster. When Moses came down from the mountain, he was furious because he discovered the people were unrestrained. When restraints are cast off, the sins of the flesh begin to come forward. This is why we keep crucifying the old sinful passions by ministering to the Lord with fasting and prayer. This enables a person to *"die daily"* as the apostle Paul spoke (1 Cor. 15:31). This is also what the Lord meant when He said, *"the ruler of this world is coming, and he has nothing in Me"* (John 14:30). Fasting and prayer keeps your life hidden in Christ with God. Base and carnal passions and desires wither and evaporate through the spiritual discipline of fasting and prayer.

The grace for fasting is given as we advance in our walk with the Lord. As I mentioned earlier, it is not always necessary to have a special leading of the Holy Spirit in order to start a fast. You can will to fast whenever there is a good time to do so. This is similar to other choices we can freely make. For instance, you can will to pray whenever you want. You don't need a supernatural leading to spend time in prayer. It's just something we should all do on a regular basis. When you are filled with the Spirit, you can pray in tongues whenever you desire to strengthen your inner man. You do not need special permission or an angelic visitation to spur you on. The apostle Paul said it well in the following verse:

> *For if I pray in a tongue, my spirit prays, but my understanding is unfruitful. What is the conclusion then? I **will** pray with the*

*spirit, and I **will** pray with the understanding* (1 Corinthians 14:14-15).

Notice Paul said, *"I **will** pray with the spirit."* Paul could exercise his will at any time and pray in the spirit. This is something he chose to do often and we can choose to do so as well. We can also choose to fast and spend extra time in prayer. You don't have to wait for someone else to give you permission. While it does require special permits, government authorization, and millions of dollars to build a nuclear reactor, you don't need any of those things to build your own spiritual nuclear reactor. There's no better time than now to start generating some heavenly power to pour out on the spiritual dry bones around you.

The Holy Spirit will not force you to do anything. Understanding this truth will help remove any fear regarding fasting. If you aim to fast for three days and only make it for two days, than you have not failed but rather have accomplished a two-day fast. Sundar Singh did not fail on a 40-day fast attempt. He succeeded on a fast lasting over 20 days that proved to be life-changing for him. Ten years ago, I did a 40-day fast and only drank apple juice. My fast was not a failure because I did not drink water only, but rather an achievement of what I considered to be an overall tremendous experience that launched me into what became a lifestyle of fasting and prayer, a more effective ministry, and most importantly a closer walk with God.

Recently I read a testimony where an older gentleman did a 40-day fast and only drank two cups of coffee each day. Some believers actually criticized him, saying it wasn't a real fast because he drank coffee. But the critics failed to see that he ate no food for 40 days! These are the religious critics who strain out a gnat but swallow a camel. Have no fear of failure when you fast, because you are already accepted by God. The Lord will supply strength to you and He will honor your desire to be closer to Him. Take one day at a time and you will be surprised how quickly all fear and apprehension will vanish.

The devil does not want you to fast and pray. He will allow all types of well-meaning but misinformed people to share their concerns with you. You will also encounter unexplainable occurrences in which people offer to take you out to eat and pay for your meal. Before, nobody would take you out and buy you a meal. But when you choose to start a fast, suddenly everyone wants to bake you a cake or order you a pizza! The grace of God will strengthen you during such trials that you may stay focused and continue on with your fast.

Whenever you deny yourself food there is a humbling of the soul that takes place. God created within our soul the ability to enjoy pleasure.

The righteous eats to the satisfying of his soul... (Proverbs 13:25).

The soul of man was created by God to enjoy the good things which He placed in the earth for us. He even put taste buds on our tongues so that we might enjoy food of all types, whether sweet and sour or hot and spicy. God takes great pleasure in the endless variety of food which He created for us to enjoy and the never-ending methods in which it may be prepared and cooked. God is very artistic and creating good food is an art in itself.

A little starvation can really do more for the average sick man than can the best medicines and the best doctors. I do not mean a restricted diet; I mean total abstinence from food. I speak from

> experience; starvation has been my cold and fever doctor for 15 years, and has accomplished a cure in all instances. —Mark Twain

As much as God takes pleasure in our food and drink, He also desires that it not go beyond its intended purpose of blessing and become an idol. Fasting with prayer allows your spirit to take its rightful place in dominance over the soul and body.

*Now may the God of peace Himself sanctify you completely; and may your whole **spirit, soul, and body** be preserved blameless at the coming of our Lord Jesus Christ* (1 Thessalonians 5:23).

The above verse is most likely the most misquoted verse in the Bible. Almost every time you hear someone quote or see it written, it is in this order—body, soul, spirit. It is often quoted in complete opposite order of how the apostle Paul listed it. This is because even most Christians live their lives in a reverse order so that their physical senses (their physical bodies) are the first area of priority. This is the realm where the apostle Thomas lived for a while, saying:

*The other disciples therefore said to him, "We have seen the Lord." So he said to them, "**Unless I see** in His hands the print of the nails, and **put my finger** into the print of the nails, and **put my hand** into His side, I will not believe"* (John 20:25).

Thomas later was filled with the Spirit (Acts 2) and went on to operate in remarkable faith and miracles. But at this time he was still operating primarily in the sense realm. In other words, if he couldn't see it, he wasn't going to believe it. When Thomas was filled with the Holy Spirit, he became a great man of faith.

I have been to his gravesite in India and also have visited the humble cave where he stayed as he ministered to the Hindus in southern India before dying as a martyr. Thomas ministered in India for 17 years, even traveling beyond northern India and into modern-day Pakistan as well as Iran. He even spent two months in China before venturing to southern India where he ministered effectively and died. He started hundreds of churches in India, two of which are still in existence today. At the cave in which he lived, there are special memorial signs listing detailed accounts of all the blind people who received sight, the number of lame who were healed, the hundreds of lepers who were made whole, the great number raised from the dead, along with statistics of other miracles performed through his anointed ministry. His apostolic ministry is one of the most historically recorded of the twelve apostles. Thomas stepped out of the realm governed by sight and emotion and moved into the faith realm.

Fasting and prayer are the cure to put the body in its proper biblical place, which is in subjection to your spirit. Others choose to put the soul (intellect) in a place of dominance over their spirit. This also is out of divine order and results in pride, arrogance, and a "know-it-all attitude." The carnal mind will put up a great resistance to the Spirit of God. Paul also spoke of this challenge.

The carnal mind is enmity [hostile] against God... (Romans 8:7).

Fasting humbles the body because the body becomes weak when it is deprived of food. Fasting humbles the soul because the soul enjoys good food, and when the pleasure of taste is deprived, the soul begins to lose its grip of dominance. The end result of fasting combined with prayer is that your spirit will rise up in power and you will operate out of the core of your very being. Base desires and carnal thoughts will wilt and pass away. What is left will be clarity and calmness. The impatience of the flesh (body) and the stubbornness of the intellect (soul) will be broken by the anointing of the Holy Spirit. The grass will appear greener, the birds' singing will sound more beautiful, your marriage and family will be more highly valued, and the Cross of Christ will be embraced with a renewed passion. Anticipate the grace of God to assist you while you fast. Have no fear of failing to complete your intended fast. God loves you and He will be very near to you during this time. With His grace you will experience the breakthrough you are looking for.

CHAPTER THREE

FOOD WHICH YOU DO NOT KNOW

DURING ONE OF HIS MANY journeys of preaching the Gospel, Jesus was traveling north from Judea to Galilee. There were two routes that could be taken, with the most direct route passing through Samaria. Jesus took the most direct route and stopped in the city of Sychar. Jesus was tired from the journey, most likely he was more fatigued than the twelve apostles because Jesus was in the habit of getting up very early to pray, often hours before the sun ever came up. He rested at a place known as Jacob's Well, which was also where Jacob had given land to his son Joseph. The twelve apostles went into the city to buy food, leaving Jesus alone with some time to rest at the well. As He rested a Samaritan woman came to draw water from the well (see John 4).

The fact that the woman came alone at noon seems unusual, because the other women typically drew their water early in the morning, usually in groups so that they could talk and share the latest news and stories. Yet this woman is alone, suggesting she was not received by the local women. Upon seeing the woman, Jesus asks her for a drink of water. She must have been surprised that He did this because it was not customary for a man to speak so openly to a woman in a public place, nor for a Jew to speak to a Samaritan.

The Lord is able to minister to this woman with the help of the Holy Spirit. Operating in the prophet's anointing, with the word of knowledge in operation, Jesus miraculously reveals the secrets of her heart, particularly that she has been formerly married five times, and the man she is living with now is not her husband. Now we have a better understanding of why she came to the well when it was not busy. Most likely she was an attractive woman, which would explain why other men would take her even after she had already been divorced multiple times before. It would also appear that the other women in the city despised her and excommunicated her, not wanting her to have an opportunity to get around their husbands and potentially wreck another marriage.

The conversation continues as the Holy Spirit softens this woman's heart, and she embraces Jesus as a prophet—and much more. When she leaves to go and tell the residents of the city about the Messiah, she is so thrilled with having met the Savior that she completely forgets her water pot!

The woman then left her waterpot, went her way into the city, and said to the men, "Come, see a Man who told me all things that I ever did. Could this be the Christ?" Then they went out of the city and came to Him (John 4:28-30).

What was before a daily chore of high priority is now overwhelmed with a love beyond anything she ever knew. God has come into her life. That which once seemed so important is now temporarily suspended due to divine intervention.

When the Spirit of God falls upon students in school, who cares about finishing the algebra equation or athletic practice? When God shows up, everything else is out the window. Let the children enjoy their God. Let the Holy Spirit have His way. Leave the water pots behind. Cancel the golf game, skip the hair salon, and receive Jesus and His Spirit of revival. Jesus only stayed in Sychar for two days. When the glory is there, you have to give God your full attention and take advantage of the moment. You can always go back later and get some water. The well was not going to disappear; it was still there when the woman later returned after the revival. When Jesus comes, He introduces you into the life of the Spirit. Water pots are left behind, excessive devotion to hobbies is abandoned, the corporate man addicted to career success is set free, and the human spirit prevails over the Adamic distractions. The lost hear the Gospel and are saved, while the believers awake from their sleep, dust themselves off from spiritual apathy, and throw off their grave clothes.

Wake up from your sleep, climb out of your coffins; Christ will show you the light! (Ephesians 5:11 MSG)

Eventually, the Lord's disciples returned from the city with food and they urged Him to eat.

But He said to them, "I have food to eat of which you do not know" (John 4:32).

This statement puzzled the disciples. The potential of this truth still puzzles many believers today. The disciples thought that perhaps someone had brought Jesus some food while they were gone. Jesus goes on to explain that there is a different type of food that can also bring nourishment and strength. The Lord's food was to do the will of the One who sent Him, and to finish the work given to Him by the Heavenly Father. This is not some mystical truth that can't be experienced today in a real way.

We can also know this reality. We can enjoy natural food, and we can also welcome a divine override of our desire for food which can be suspended for a higher cause, an eternal purpose. There is a place in Christ where our spiritual hunger can swallow up natural appetite and desire.

We have seen that when Jesus shows up, water pots are left behind, fisherman leave their nets, tax collectors walk away from lucrative wealth, and the Kingdom of God takes its proper place of preeminence in the lives of men and women, boys and girls. There are others as well throughout church history who left their water pots and realized that Christ Jesus can be all-sustaining. Padre Pio from Italy was one such man who had a proven and effective prophetic ministry spanning over 50 years in the early twentieth century, in which miracles were normal and Jesus was followed with wholehearted devotion. Such devotion can often affect one's eating habits as the Spirit of God grants unusual graces to the spiritually hungry. Padre Pio was born in 1887. By the time he died in 1968, he was receiving 5,000 letters a month and had visitors from all over the world. Padre Pio enjoyed food but often was so consumed with his pursuit of God that he never ate much. The following story is shared concerning his eating habits.

> Despite his increasing weight, Padre Pio was anything but a hearty eater. A physician who examined him and noted his weight at one hundred ninety-eight pounds also insisted that his daily caloric intake was less than his weight! The only meal he took in the refectory was the midday dinner. Even then, according to Dr. Sala, Padre Pio "took only forkfuls of food," not nearly enough to "support his body". Don Giorgio Pogany likewise recalled, "No human being could live with that amount of food that Padre Pio ate. He ate almost nothing." Padre

Giovanni of Baggio insisted that Pio ate "perhaps a fifth of the amount eaten by a normal man." Father Dominic, who sat next to him at the table, in response to an article that claimed that Padre Pio lived on a diet consisting of but a few mouthfuls of vegetables and a few sips of lemon juice, wrote, "He eats also macaroni, cheese, peas, beans, fruit, liver, etc., and, as all good Italians, he drinks a glass of wine." He also occasionally enjoyed fried sausage and dried ham. But everything was eaten in minute quantities, and frequently he handed much of the food that was served to him to the men sitting next to him. When he handed his plate to the equally abstemious Father Dominic, who invariably protested, Pio would smile and say, "Corragio!"—"Courage!"

Even considering the fact that Padre Pio obtained very little exercise, what he ate was, according to the testimony of every doctor who observed him, insufficient to keep an adult alive, let alone to account for his robust appearance. Moreover, there were several occasions when, ill with a stomach virus, he took nothing for several days but sips of water, yet nevertheless gained weight. On one such occasion, Dr. Sanguinetti noted, with amazement, that his patient gained six pounds after an eight day siege of illness during which he could hold down only a small amount of water. He asked Pio how he could possibly gain weight when fasting. "Assimilation," Pio insisted. "Everything depends on assimilation."

"But, there is nothing to assimilate if you don't eat."

"Well, every morning I take Communion."

"No, you're not convincing me," said the doctor. "You must be hiding food somewhere, so as to trick me."

"I haven't eaten anything, just as you have seen. But we must think of the parable in the Bible about the sower. The grain fell on good ground and produced a hundredfold. You see that my soil is good and I have produced much."

"Very well," said the physician. "These are spiritual things. What does the spirit have to do with the body?"

Padre Pio went on to say that he was nourished solely by the Eucharist (Communion). "It is the Lord who does this and not I. It is the Lord who is working in me."[1]

When you have a strong prayer life like Padre Pio and you combine that with a fasting lifestyle, then you move into the realm of ongoing miracles. The following example is just one of the many miracles that happened throughout his anointed ministry.

Dr. Sanguinetti told me about another incident, which he personally witnessed. One day a woman came to San Giovanni Rotondo with a wicker suitcase. She went into the church and waited in line to go to confession with the other women. When it was her turn, she opened the suitcase in front of Padre Pio and broke out in tears. Wrapped in some old clothing in the suitcase was the body of a baby that was about six months old. The woman was coming to San Giovanni Rotondo with her sick son, hoping that Padre Pio would heal him. But the boy died on the train. The woman, who was overcome with anguish but still had immense faith, hid the child in her suitcase and continued on with her journey. Dr. Sanguinetti told me that if the child had been hidden in the suitcase while he was still alive, he would have certainly died from suffocation. Therefore, there was no doubt that the child was dead when she opened her suit-case for Padre Pio.

As the woman cried out in desperation, Padre Pio took the little body in his hands and prayed for a few moments. Then he turned to the mother and asked her with a firm voice, "Why are you yelling so much? Don't you see that your son is sleeping?" The woman looked at the baby and realized that he was tranquilly breathing."[2]

Prayer and fasting will open wide the prophetic realm and allow you to experience the wonders of Heaven. I have had many supernatural experiences, not because I am a minister, but because of an effort to diligently seek the Lord. God is no respecter of persons. Prayer and fasting will cause your spiritual eyes to be anointed to see. The reason some are quick to criticize supernatural experiences is because they do not understand the prophetic realm. This is the realm of God, angels, redeemed saints, and other sights that the Holy Spirit may choose to reveal to you, including hell and the demonic realm. Don't put limits on God. Be open to biblical experiences even if they haven't happened to you yet. The Holy Spirit wants to anoint your prophetic understanding.

Once I was in Jerusalem for a ministry conference. I was one of the guest speakers, but the week was almost over and I had finished my sessions, so I could now relax and sit on the front row knowing my work was done. Another dear minister friend of mine in his seventies had also finished his last session, so we were sitting next to one another on the front row. This man next to me was known internationally as a true apostle who had been involved in spearheading many moves of God. As we both sat on the front row, a prophet friend of ours from India took the pulpit for his final session of ministry. This prophet, who operated in the gifts of the Spirit, was one of the sharpest prophets I had ever met in my life. As he ministered the good Word of God, we all sat and enjoyed his blessed message.

However, while sitting there I soon began to experience an unusual tingling sensation on my head. I reached up with my hand and gently brushed my hair and small flakes of manna began to fall off and drop to the floor. I initially thought, "Hmmm, I've never had a problem with dandruff. I wonder what these white flakes are?" The more I touched my hair the more the manna from Heaven kept materializing and then falling to the floor. Because there were hundreds of people sitting behind me, I didn't want to make a scene so I tried to just sit still and see if it would go away.

Within a minute or so the manna disappeared, and then I felt a warm liquid being poured on top of my head. It felt like warm oil was being poured all over me. It tickled, so I reached up and noticed my head and hair were dripping with oil. The outpouring didn't stop as the oil began to run down over my face and started dripping on my shirt. Throughout the entire message as I sat there the oil continued to flow at a steady pace. Toward the end of the message, my head and hair were soaked with some type of pure oil that felt like olive oil.

Leaning over to my minister friend next to me, I whispered so as not to disrupt the preaching or those around me, and said, "Hey, there's oil being poured on my head. I'm trying to figure out what's going on."

He softly laughed and with an expression of delight he quietly said, "Yes, something is taking place. A few minutes ago I was sitting here and looked to my side and I noticed wings pop out of my back! Suddenly I flew straight up and was carried in the spirit realm to the palace of Ashtoreth. She has a palace that is jet black in color and she was running around in great anger because many saints are breaking free from her power of lust. Her palace seemed to be in a state of panic and pandemonium. When you spoke to me I had just returned from have been translated in the Spirit to that place and back."

Just about that time the prophet who was preaching finished his message. A line quickly formed as people began to come forward to have him lay his hands upon them. This doesn't often happen, but one of the head assistants placed me and the minister next to me in the prayer line. We decided to go with the flow so we stood there in the line and eventually the prophet worked his way to us. He reached my minister friend first and began to immediately prophesy over him, "Thus says the Lord: this day the Lord has given unto you wings that you may ascend into the second heaven to behold the strategies and plans of the enemy." Other words were also spoken, but the prophet hit the nail right on the head.

Next, he came to me and prophesied, "Thus says the Lord: the Prophet Elijah has been standing in the meeting the whole service and has been pouring oil over your head. You will go to new countries next year, and creative miracles will become normal in your ministry. You will have a great ministry." After the service we talked further and this prophet further shared with me that the anointing of oil upon my life by Elijah was for the purpose of operating in creative miracles, just as Elijah did in his earthly ministry.

Well, the next year I did go and minister in four new countries that I had never set foot in before. We are also seeing the creative miracles become normal in every service. Even last Sunday as I ministered, a young girl with a completely deaf left ear had her hearing made whole as she heard with brilliant clarity for the first time. After the service the girl's mother told me that not only was the ear deaf, but that the doctors who previously examined the ear said there were parts missing, thus making it impossible to ear. So, this was not just a healing that took place, but rather a miracle of healing which involved God creating and putting new parts in that were not there before.

Prayer is not the easiest thing in the world. Prayer is the hardest thing in the world. Prayer is the most demanding thing in the world. I had the pleasure of praying very often with Duncan Campbell, a man God used in the Hebrides revival, 1950 onward. I asked him one day about a certain event, he said, "Yes, that's right. When I was ministering the place was like iron; it seemed as though God was a million miles away. And my message was like throwing a rubber ball at the wall; my words came back on me." In front of him were all kinds of ministers, but he didn't say anything to the preachers and the deacons and the elders. He pointed to a boy sitting over there, called him by name and said, "Laddie, will you pray?" A sixteen year old high school boy!

And he stood up, and he said in his Scottish way, "Ach, what is the good of praying if we are not right with God?" And he began to quote Psalm 24, "Who shall ascend into the hill of the Lord? He that hath clean hands and pure heart," and so forth and so on.

"And when he'd finished," Duncan told me, "The stillness of eternity was on the building."

And the boy prayed 10 minutes, 20 minutes, 30 minutes, 40 minutes, 45 minutes. And then, when he prayed as though he could see the invisible he said, "Satan." Oh, I've heard people say this almost facetiously in some meetings, "Get the Devil out of this place." The young boy stood there and said, "Satan, I rebuke you. Get out of this territory! In the name of the Father and the Son and the Holy Ghost. I plead the blood of Christ, *be gone!*"

And just as though a switch was pulled in Heaven God came on the meeting, He came on a tavern at the end of the road and people left it. He came on a dance at the end of the road and people left it. We have to drag people to the altar; there are no altar calls in the New Testament if you want to be *really* scriptural. Altar calls are an invention for when the Holy Ghost doesn't deal with people. This boy prayed, the Holy Ghost came and that whole community vibrated with God. —Leonard Ravenhill

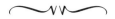

Through regular prayer and fasting, the spiritual gifts and callings become activated. The prophetic realm becomes normal, and you function as in a way to excel in everyday, normal activities while also blending seamlessly with the supernatural dimension. The domain of Heaven is no longer some faraway place that can never be glimpsed at or seen. The spiritual walk is revealed through prophetic experiences that God chooses to grant. God grants access to those who pursue Him with all their heart. As I have traveled around the globe over the years, I have met and talked with many prophets who passionately seek the Lord. One common experience of many of them is that they have seen Heaven and have met some of the saints and angels who dwell there. The prophets who experience such visions are those who have not been conformed to the limitations that are often placed upon the western church regarding supernatural experiences. One must be open to the fullness of God's word. If Paul was caught up into Heaven, then it can happen to other believers as well (see 2 Cor. 12:2-4).

On Christmas Eve of 2010, very early in the morning the Lord gave me a wonderful prophetic experience—a Christmas present that I wasn't expecting. Kelly and I and our youngest daughter, Abigail, had flown from North Carolina to Tulsa, Oklahoma to spend Christmas with our oldest daughter and her husband, as well as to prepare for the New Year's Eve Prophetic Conference, which my ministry was hosting in Tulsa. Although it was Christmastime and there was wonderful food everywhere, I had set my heart to fast and pray for the upcoming meeting. This proved difficult to do because I was surrounded constantly by frosted sugar cookies, lemon cake, pies, and an endless assortment of delicious meats. When we fast and pray the Lord sees the sacrifice we make. Our fasting from food combined with prayer conveys a strong message to the Lord that our desire to have our voice heard on high is stronger than the desire to eat. The Lord highly values any sacrifice that we make to Him. I fasted for several days before Christmas and then ate the traditional Christmas meal with my family. After that meal I fasted for five more days leading up to the New Year's meeting.

On Christmas Eve I found it very difficult to sleep. Perhaps it was because of being in a bed that I wasn't used to, but whatever the reason, I was awake most of the night. At 4:30 in the morning while still lying in bed, I went into a vision and was caught up to Heaven in Paradise where the Lord Jesus was waiting for me. Paul mentions that there are multiple levels in Heaven.

> *I know a man in Christ who fourteen years ago—whether in the body I do not know, or whether out of the body I do not know, God knows—such a one was caught up to the* **third heaven**. *And I know such a man—whether in the body or out of the body I do not know, God knows—how he was caught up into* **Paradise** *and heard inexpressible words, which it is not lawful for a man to utter* (2 Corinthians 12:2-4).

Upon my arrival in Paradise, the Lord Jesus smiled at me and asked me to sit down on a park bench that appeared to be made of solid gold. As I sat there, Jesus slowly stepped behind me and the sight in front of me changed. I now found myself sitting on a park bench in Southern California. Before my sight, a group of about seventy people began to pass by me, on their way to a certain location. Somehow I knew the people were unsaved, most of them looked like hippies, and it was obvious they had no interest in Jesus Christ. When I asked them where they were going, they replied, "We are going shopping to buy clothes." Their response reminded me of how consumed many people are with the cares of the world.

The Lord's words from the Gospel of Matthew echoed in my ears, "And why do you worry about clothes? Learn how the wildflowers of the field grow: they don't labor or spin thread. Yet I tell you that not even Solomon in all his splendor was adorned like one of these! If that's how God clothes the grass of the field, which is here today and thrown into the furnace tomorrow, won't He do much more for you—you of little faith?" (See Matthew 6:28-30.)

The sight of the small group passing by with no hope and no joy in life prompted within me a desire to share the Lord's salvation message to them. But how could I when anything related to

God seemed so offensive to them? Not only that, but I was out numbered seventy to one, and I was on their turf. The spiritual darkness on the people was so strong that the only way to break through to them would be by the power of the Holy Spirit.

As I sat on the park bench watching these people pass by, I was again returned to the golden bench in Heaven where the Lord was waiting for me. He sensed my desire to share the Gospel with these people on earth. The Lord also read my thoughts of how I didn't want to offend them with a typical "religious appeal." As I sat on the park bench in Heaven, the Lord said to me, "This man will help you reach them." When He said that, a man walked across a golden street toward me, smiling. He appeared to be about thirty years old with light-colored brown hair. This person was someone I recognized from photos, having vaguely heard about him in my personal studies of modern-day church history. I had read some articles describing his anointed ministry, but also knew of his character flaws which eventually ended his ministry and shortened his life, so I was surprised to see him in Heaven. The man was Lonnie Frisbee.

Lonnie Frisbee was a man greatly used by God during the Jesus Movement of the late 1960s and early 1970s. Known by many as the original "Jesus Freak," he was raised in a broken home and was sexually abused when he was a young boy. He then engaged in heavy drug use and at the age of 15 entered the underground gay community while also merging into the hippie lifestyle. He was later converted while having a vision in which Jesus appeared to him. He gave his heart to Jesus and was cleansed from all his sin.

Immediately upon his conversion, he began winning souls right and left. He was chosen by God as a catalyst for the Jesus Movement, was strongly influential in the birth of Calvary Chapel, and later demonstrated the power of the Spirit in a way that triggered the worldwide growth of the Vineyard churches. Although his ministry brought him international notoriety—such as him being featured on the cover of *Time* and other magazines—he privately struggled with overcoming his fleshly tendencies of staying morally pure. In some ways he was like a Samson, having a powerful anointing to operate in the Spirit, but never fulfilling his full destiny because of not "dying daily" as the apostle Paul exhorted all believers to do (see 1 Cor. 15:31). Even so, he is in Heaven today just as Samson is, and we can learn from the positive examples of his life.

As Lonnie Frisbee walked toward me, he said with a smile, "This is the way to do it." He laid his hands on me, imparting an apostolic boldness as the Spirit of God then came upon me like a lion. Suddenly, I was back on the earth sitting on the park bench. I jumped up and ran to the front of the group of people and began talking to them about Jesus. As they kept walking forward, I was walking backward so that I could directly face them while talking to them. The boldness of the Spirit was so strong on me that I started putting my hands on their foreheads, and although they didn't like it, they didn't try to stop me either. It reminded me of giving a child a spoonful of medicine. The child doesn't want to receive it because it doesn't taste good, but at the same time they know it's what they need because they are sick, so they are willing to swallow it.

I kept laying my hands on them while smiling and talking to them as we walked. As I was doing this the Shekinah glory of God began to come down upon the group and myself. It got so strong that all of our legs began to get weaker and weaker, till eventually we all collapsed on the ground, overcome by the Spirit of God. It was then that each person was mightily convicted by the Holy Spirit, resulting in every person giving their heart to the Lord and receiving Jesus into their heart.

The next moment I was back in Heaven. I could see that Lonnie Frisbee was walking away toward a beautiful park as the Lord Jesus appeared and stepped toward me. He said, "Those who I call to operate in My Spirit's revival power are those who must fully trust in Me. I do not choose as man chooses, but I choose vessels the world deems as foolish and worthless. Often such vessels have inherent weaknesses, of which I am aware, and I deliberately choose these vessels because of their human frailty. To overcome they must continually rely on My strength and grace. The greater the anointing and the greater the glory, the greater one's reliance must rest upon Me. I can fill any vessel with My Spirit's power if they humbly seek Me with all their heart."

I stood there thinking about the Lord's words while still feeling surges of the Spirit's power going through me from the previous experience. I could sense that the Lord took great delight in Lonnie, knowing that while on earth he had gained a level of walking in the Spirit's power that very few achieve. The Lord does not see him as a failure, but as one of His children made clean and spotless by His blood. There are no dirty or guilty saints in Heaven. The Lord looked at me and smiled. His face was so full of compassion and kindness. He said, "You know the necessary steps to come into My last-days anointing which I desire for you to walk in. The coming outpouring will eclipse all previous moves of My Spirit."

"Yes, Lord," I replied, "it's just that it's so difficult at times. Only by Your grace can I walk this path; it seems to require everything within me to stay focused and not be distracted."

"The sacrifices indeed are great," the Lord replied, "but well worth the end results." There was a twinkle in His eye as He said this. He then took what looked like a small book and held it in His hand before me. I knew the book contained "necessary steps" that Jesus requires of one to operate in the anticipated end-time release of His glory. The book appeared to be about seventy pages and was about the size of my hand. He then took the book and plunged it into my heart. His hand and the book went right into me. Chapters with short articles were instantly revealed to my spirit. I could see chapters called "Apostolic Boldness," "Explosive Power Through Prayer and Fasting," "Israel, the Jew, and You," "Be Perfect as Your Father in Heaven Is Perfect," along with the corresponding texts. Each message was short, only a few pages in length and straight to the point, nothing complicated or hard to understand. There were other chapters as well, each one being a key to walking in the power of the Spirit and understanding how to reap the great harvest of souls that lies before us.

He then stepped back and said to me, "I have called you for the work of revival. You will operate in the power of My Spirit and show forth My glory with signs and wonders. Stay humble, stay in the prayer closet, for you will bring many into My Kingdom. Go now, My son, and hasten to the work which I have called you to do!" With those words a deep joy filled my heart, along with a divine empowerment to carry on with renewed strength.

After the Lord spoke those words, I at once found myself back lying on the bed in Tulsa. Usually I don't open Christmas presents until the sun comes up, but this one sure came early. I stayed awake and prayed for a while, then got a little more rest before getting up and celebrating Christmas with the family. That morning I shared the vision I had received with my family. It sure was interesting when my son-in-law Alex opened his gift from his wife Jennifer. His gift was the biggest present under the tree. When he opened it we all laughed as we saw that he had been given a super-deluxe Frisbee golf set. God has a sense of humor, as I also received a Frisbee related gift as well!

Following that visitation, I won more souls for the Lord that year than in any year before in my ministry. With a new boldness, I would reach out to the lost souls in my meetings, not wanting any to perish, and I have since not stopped in my efforts to reach the lost on an ongoing basis. Doing so has never made me happier before in my life. God is so good. When we sacrifice and push back the plate in order to take extra time for prayer, God rewards us openly and liberally.

When we give the Lord our best He will and can reward us in many different ways. Sometimes these rewards are visits to Heaven that the Lord gives to us when we face discouragement or sorrow. When our family dog passed away at eleven years of age, my wife and I were very sad. Our dog's name was Tabitha and she was an Airedale terrier. Before we bought her we waited and prayed for two years, wanting to have a special pet. After two years, we knew the kind of dog we wanted so we researched and found a kennel that carried Airedale terriers.

It was in the middle of winter when we arrived at the kennel, having been informed that there were several puppies that we could choose from. We were very disappointed in the kennel because the dogs were not well taken care of. The puppies were covered with mud and were placed outside in temperatures that were in the low 20s. While the puppies did seem to be happy despite their rough living conditions, Kelly happened to notice one puppy that sat in a corner of the kennel all by itself. This puppy was very beautiful even though it was dirty, cold, and wet and appeared to be sad and lonely. You can guess which puppy Kelly picked out.

As soon as Kelly saw that sad little puppy she said, "This one is going to be ours, and her name will be Tabitha." We took that sweet little puppy home and bathed it in warm water and then took it to a vet to receive its proper vaccinations. This dog soon became a great source of joy for the whole family. For years we traveled full-time in the ministry in a motor home. We traveled from meeting to meeting, crossing many states and covering countless miles. Each night when traveling, we would park for the night in a different place. Our dog Tabitha always slept by the door of the motor home as a guard dog. Many potential situations of theft or wrongdoing were thwarted by her alertness, keen sense, and loud bark.

God will either give you what you ask, or something far better. —Robert Murray McCheyne

Tabitha was very special to us because we spent so much time together. Sadly, we had to put her to sleep at the age of eleven because of severe arthritis, hip problems, and the constant pain associated with these illnesses. For several days Kelly and I were sad over Tabitha's departure. We still carried on with our necessary work, but our hearts were heavy because of Tabitha being gone.

Five days after I took Tabitha to the vet to have her put to sleep, I was preaching in a meeting being hosted by my ministry. We had a wonderful service and I was just about to close the meeting when the Spirit of God came upon me, and I went into an open vision and could see clearly into Heaven. The vision came so suddenly, so unexpectedly, it was like a large movie screen had been lowered down from above for me to watch. Before my eyes I saw the most beautiful park with towering pine trees, flowing streams, and majestic mountains in the background. There were thousands upon thousands of dogs running around and playing happily. I could see a hill with a single dog sitting on top of it. As I focused my eyes I clearly saw Tabitha on grass so green and lush that no golf course on earth could rival it.

Gone from Tabitha were the crippling arthritis, hip problems, and even old age. She appeared in the prime of her life, looking similar in some ways to a regal lion. While I was looking at her, the Lord walked up and stood next to Tabitha. She had a beautiful collar around her neck and a leash extended about three feet from the collar, which was suspended in midair. The Lord Jesus then appeared in the vision standing next to Tabitha. He looked at me and smiled, and said, "Do you see this?" as he pointed to the dog leash.

"Yes, Lord," I replied.

He snapped his fingers and said, "These don't exist here," as the leash suddenly disappeared before my sight. Just at that time one of the many angels in the heavenly dog park threw a tennis ball and Tabitha took off chasing it with great delight.

After spending some time watching the myriad of dogs play, I was then carried in the Spirit to my heavenly mansion. It appeared there was a shift in activities, as if the day was drawing to a close and people were settling in within their homes for a relaxing evening. There was not night or even the slightest hint of a shadow, but it was more like a change in colors that went from bright and brilliant to more of a soft light that presented a mood of worship, contemplation, and holy reverence.

I was taken into a part of my mansion where the reading room is located. Against the walls stood mahogany bookshelves with books neatly stacked that were bound with rich leather covers. The floor was a warm-colored polished stone with a beautiful marble texture. The furniture was beautiful—with luxurious chairs and several couches in cloth material made from colors of red, gold, and purple. The furniture looked so inviting to sit in. Fresh flowers were in well-placed crystal vases that sat on exquisite pedestals and tables.

A large stone fireplace with a beautiful wooden mantle was positioned as a focal point in the room. The mantle was made of some exotic looking wood and was polished to a deep shine. A fire was lit and was gently burning, giving off a warm and comforting heat. The closest earthly description that I could reference my mansion to would be the Biltmore Mansion in Asheville, North Carolina. I have visited there before and it is truly a well-built earthly mansion. But in Heaven everything is on such a higher level that it's hard to describe the beauty. In Heaven everything appears to be brand-new. Nothing is broken or ever needs to be repaired. There are no inconsistencies to be found. Even if you go to Disney World or stay in five-star luxury hotels eventually you will see trash or some type of imperfection. The level of upkeep and perfection is consistent throughout all of Heaven.

Most importantly, in Heaven the presence and glory of God are everywhere. The peace of God fills every square inch of Heaven. The glory of God is in the fabric of the furniture, it's in the plants in the garden, and it's in the fragrance that the flowers emit. The glory of God is even in the air you breathe.

As I stood there quietly looking around the room I saw Tabitha lying in the center of the room in front of the warm fireplace. She lay asleep on a thick rug that looked as if it were made from lamb's wool. It was then that I could see her collar more clearly. It was made of polished gold and in exquisite cursive lettering it had her name written, saying, "Tabitha Brooks." The love of God filled my heart. Truly God created us to live for eternity with pleasure and joy forevermore.

When the vision ended, I found I was the only one left in the building; everyone had gone home. My wife had locked things up and driven home. Upon looking at my watch I noticed that over one hour had passed, although it seemed like I had been on my knees for only ten minutes. Upon driving home that night I was again mindful of God's eternal Kingdom and the value of serving Him in this life with our whole hearts. When we do, God will reward us. He will feed us with hidden manna from His own hand, and we will soar like eagles and be sustained by His presence. As you seek God through prayer and fasting, the prophetic realm will unfold before you and you will eat from the Lord's Table. The food that others *do not know* will be your daily bread. Your joy will be full, your God will be real to you, and you will walk like Jesus in the earth.

Endnotes

1. Bernard Ruffin, *Padre Pio: The True Story* (Huntington, IN: Our Sunday Visitor, 1991), Chapter 26. (Used with permission.)

2. Renzo Allegri, *Padre Pio: A Man of Hope* (Ann Arbor, MI: Charis Books, 2000), 207. (Used with permission.)

CHAPTER FOUR

GENERATING THERMONUCLEAR ENERGY AND HEAT

IT IS IMPORTANT TO SPEND as much time as possible in prayer during your fast. If you fail to pray while fasting, than all you are accomplishing is an extreme diet. Prayers that are associated with fasting usually involve strong intercession that is based on taking hold of the promises of God. While many people fast to draw near to God, which is a noble and just cause, there is also plenty of biblical precedence for fasting due to crisis situations and urgent needs. This is what took place with Esther when she called for a three-day fast from food and water for all the Jews due to the life-threatening situation that was sprung on them by evil Haman (see Esther 4:16). If you are facing critical circumstances that jeopardize you and those you love, you need to turn to God with fasting and intercessory prayer. Don't expect someone else to do your praying and fasting for you. Take charge of your life and rise up and respond bravely.

There are many different types of prayer, just as there are many different types of sports. To govern games of sport properly, there are different rules for the various sports. The designated rules for basketball do not apply for soccer. In the same sense, the spiritual laws governing prayers to God revolving around fellowship and communion are different from those which concern prayers of strong intercession.

Prayers of intimacy with God are often quiet, contemplative, and are over an extended period of time where prayers are not only offered up, but there is a waiting to listen and hear what the Lord's response will be. We see a good example of this with Habakkuk, who in prayer pleaded his case to the Lord and then patiently waited for the Lord's answer (see Hab. 2:1). The Lord did speak to him, but the answer that came was different from what Habakkuk was expecting.

Intercessory prayer is different from devotional prayer. Devotional prayer keeps our walk with the Lord vibrant and fresh. From this level we springboard from the heart of God and begin to passionately pray for those promptings that He places within us. Intercessory prayer moves us into the territory of groaning and travailing in the Spirit. This level of praying is highly effective at moving the hand of God, as demonstrated in the life of Elijah.

> *The effective, fervent prayer of a righteous man avails much. Elijah was a man with a nature like ours, and he prayed earnestly that it would not rain; and it did not rain on the land for three years and six months. And he prayed again, and the heaven gave rain, and the earth produced its fruit* (James 5:16-18).

The Bible tells us that Elijah prayed in an effective way. The New Testament Greek word *effective* is our English word for *energy*. Elijah prayed with energy. It also says that his prayers were "fervent." This is the Greek word for *heat*. So, we see that God answered the prayers of Elijah as he prayed with energy and heat. Have you ever been to a prayer meeting where there was no energy or heat? You leave with a sense that not much was accomplished. Very little was achieved because with intercessory prayer you have to operate in the rules that God established for this type of praying in order to get positive results. If you don't follow the rules of praying with energy and heat, then you won't see results.

Sometimes we have had visitors drop into our church prayer meetings. It's interesting to see the expressions on the faces of visitors who have only been in traditional prayer meetings where people sit in a circle, pray in hushed tones, and just hope that maybe God will hear their prayers. In some churches, the prayer meetings should really be labeled gossip meetings. The church members supposedly come to pray but feel the need each time to discuss the "dirty laundry" that they have heard over the past week. Others come to "prayer meeting," but after prolonged fellowship and random talk they eventually get around to praying a few minutes until someone walks over to the piano and begins to lead the prayer group in worship songs. Again, this is not prayer. It's so easy to do everything under the sun but pray.

When the praying starts at our church, guests are surprised to see they have walked into a fully-functioning spiritual nuclear reactor. There's heat, there's energy, and there's nobody sitting in a group holding hands softly singing "Kumbaya." There's nobody on the keyboard or guitar. We come to pray, not play and horse around, which is why God is doing mighty works among us.

The true church lives and moves and has its being in prayer. —Leonard Ravenhill

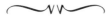

Elijah became such a giant in the history of Israel that over time he was placed on a spiritual level that was not deemed attainable for "normal" people. This is why the apostle James took extra effort to state that Elijah was a man with a nature like ours. We see in the Scriptures the reality of Elijah's humanity, that at times he was discouraged, even somewhat narrow-minded. But God worked through him mightily and answered his prayers because he followed the spiritual rules regarding successful intercessory prayer.

What are the spiritual rules of successful intercessory prayer? The Bible tells it to us plainly. According to James, we are told that Elijah prayed effectively, fervently, and earnestly. In other words, he prayed with Spirit-empowered energy and vigor, fervency and heat, and persevering continuance with intensity. We are then told that this type of praying avails much. It could also be said that this type of praying has much force, is strong, and prevails.

In like manner, if we pray using the proper rules we will also enjoy the fruitful results acquired through our anointed prayers of intercession. Don't be afraid to put your full heart into your prayers. Lean into prayer with a determined effort. Expend some energy. If after one hour of praying you don't feel like you expended anything, then you aren't drawing deep enough from the well. Have you ever been to Jerusalem to the Western Wall? It's enlightening to watch the way the Jews pray. Some will stand in front of the wall and sway their entire bodies while they pray with great zeal. When you pray like that for a solid hour and put energy into it, then you won't need to go to an aerobics class later! It's also impossible to fall asleep when moving with such vigor.

Prepare your mind to win as you enter the prayer meeting, just as you would if you were walking onto the court to compete in a big game. Show up early, show up hungry, and be aggressive with attaining the promises of God for your family, church, and community. Step up your game and give it everything you have. Then watch as you see the Lord move to answer even the most challenging situations. All things are possible with God. Pray in faith and expect miracles.

Once I was in a conversation with a very ultra-religious person and the conversation drifted to the topic of prayer. As we talked for a few minutes, the man soon stopped and with a startled look said to me, "From the way you talk you sound as if you actually think God is going to answer your prayers!" To him prayer was only a formality, a religious routine that was only done to impress others in public, but never done in faith. Believe, expect, and confess that your prayers will prevail and that you will receive from God. Be bold in your faith. The bolder you are the better the results you will get. The apostle James has conveyed to us the great expectancy and the ease of availability that we have with prayer. It's up to us to make good use of it, especially when we fast.

Many believers have never realized that it is possible to shift gears in your manner of praying. What I mean is that if you feel like you are not pressing through, it is possible to push yourself to a higher level. We see this in the following Scripture.

> *And He was withdrawn from them about a stone's throw, and He knelt down and prayed, saying, "Father, if it is Your will, take this cup away from Me; nevertheless not My will, but Yours, be done." Then an angel appeared to Him from heaven, strengthening Him. And being in agony, **He prayed more earnestly**. Then His sweat became like great drops of blood falling down to the ground* (Luke 22:41-44).

When Jesus began praying in the Garden of Gethsemane, he was praying strongly and with passion, so much so that He was sweating profusely. He had still not "prayed through" to the peace which He was seeking. God sent an angel to strengthen Him, and because of this He was able to shift to a higher gear, as it says *"He prayed **more** earnestly."* It was at this point that His sweat became like great drops of blood, and that, without question, is some heavy-duty praying. Sometimes prayer seems effortless, other times it can be as if we are in an all-out war with tremendous resistance attempting to hinder us when we pray. When there is great hindrance occurring at pivotal times, we then must break through, keeping in mind that you have the potential to go to an advanced level by shifting gears. If necessary God can also send an angel to assist you in your praying just like He did for Jesus. This type of praying can be physically exhausting, but the euphoria that comes from having prevailed through prayer is indescribable.

Our church once faced a specific need that could only be met through God's divine intervention. For several months we prayed for this need to be met as we gathered together for corporate prayer. For two months it seemed as if every time we prayed regarding this need, our prayers were being ineffective. But we kept fervently praying and refused to let the enemy deny us the blessing intended by God, even though sometimes after our time of prayer we all felt physically depleted and emotionally drained. But after two months of earnest prayer we hit the gusher one night as we all prayed together. For over one hour we were all swept along by the Spirit of God as we prayed in unity with a great joy. The best way I could describe it would be like an experience of drinking a sparkling non-alcoholic champagne. We all kept bubbling up with joy and uncontrollable laughter as we all knew we had broken through and God had answered our specific prayer. Within one week the church cried and rejoiced when I announced God had performed the miracle we petitioned Him for.

I wish all of our prayer meetings were bubbly and joyful, but sometimes there is the labor and travail that must be endured. When the miracle is birthed, then there is always time for rejoicing and celebrating. God is so good. He is not trying to hold back any good thing from His people. He has given us the privilege of exercising our spiritual authority by using the Name of Jesus and claiming the promises of His Word as our legal right and inheritance.

When you pray and fast you want to follow the Lord's guidelines, so that you are most effective in seeking God. It has always been encouraging to me that if I fast and pray properly then He will reward me openly.

Moreover, when you fast, do not be like the hypocrites, with a sad countenance. For they disfigure their faces that they may appear to men to be fasting. Assuredly, I say to you, they have their reward. But you, when you fast, anoint your head and wash your face, so that you do not appear to men to be fasting, but to your Father who is in the secret place, and your Father who sees in secret will reward you openly (Matthew 6:16-18).

You need to constantly be mindful that God will, without a doubt, reward you through seeking Him. The reward we are looking for is that our prayer, which we are specifically seeking to be answered, will be granted by the Father. Can you imagine putting yourself through a grueling fast and all you get out of it is a pat on the back or someone saying, "You sure must be a holy person because of your fasting." Jesus told us that outward recognition would be all those religiously deceived people would receive from their fasting. I don't know about you, but I'm not involved in this just to get a pat on the back or some type of religious adulation. Going without food is not something we do for fun. We are looking for our reward, which is to see our prayers answered.

Prayer will make a man cease from sin, or sin will entice a man to cease from prayer. —John Bunyon

When fasting, I try to the best of my ability to not let others know what I am doing. I always let my wife know because she prepares the meals, so I must inform her, but I endeavor to keep it hidden from others. Sometimes close friends will ask me, "You appear to have lost weight; are you fasting?" If they directly ask I will tell them, but I try to avoid going into detail regarding how long and other particulars. When doing a corporate fast that is joined by other church members and ministry partners, I have to make it public regarding the intended length of the fast so that we are all of one heart and are on the same page together. But most of the fasting I do is personal and private. Knowing that God will bring an open reward is a great motivator. Fasting and prayer requires great sacrifice. If there were not a promise of a reward then we would all lose heart. We can thank God that we can have a bold expectancy to receive the miracle we desire.

Elijah was a normal man like us. He prayed with great energy and faith and God answered his prayer. It was at Elijah's word that the heavens did not open up for three and a half years. This must have been an incredible famine that Israel experienced due to their sin and idolatry. What would happen in America if it did not rain for that long? It would wreck the economy of the country. But Elijah prayed again and the rain came pouring down, causing the land to be fruitful again.

Sadly, I have heard some ministers in their sermons greatly diminish the power of prayer and fasting. These are the same preachers who spend the day before Sunday out on the golf course and only want to have fun. Despite their well-polished messages and beautiful sanctuaries, they still have no real power. Their only power lies in their organizational ability and marketing skills. But there are no mighty miracles taking place because the Holy Spirit produces these only through lives that are centered in prayer with fasting.

So he answered and said to me: "This is the word of the Lord to Zerubbabel: 'Not by might, nor by power, but by My Spirit,' says the Lord of hosts" (Zechariah 4:6)

The following is a statement sometimes used regarding fasting that people have taken out of context. "Fasting does not change God. He is the same before you fast, when you fast, and after you fast." There have been times when I have used these very same words. From a technical standpoint this statement is true, but this truth is often cast in a negative way by some to mistakenly suggest that because God doesn't change, it is therefore pointless to fast. So, I would like to expand on this statement and add the following insight. It is true that the character of God never changes, but it is possible for God to change His heart regarding certain matters. Our prayerful actions can influence the outcome of certain situations that can cause God to intervene and change the normal course of things. It doesn't mean God's character has changed, it simply denotes our fasting combined with prayer can be very influential in touching the heart of God. There are times when the Holy Spirit may emphasize within our hearts the need for specific prayer and fasting. To ignore the inner witness given by the Holy Spirit to pray and fast is like driving past the last town which has a gas station when your fuel is already getting close to being empty and there are no other gas stations for a hundred miles. You are risking failure.

If fasting is not necessary, then why did Jesus, Paul, the twelve apostles, and the Old Testament prophets fast? God's character is never going to change. When we fast properly, we are changed and renewed by the Spirit and become more Christ-like. Prayer with fasting allows us to step into a place of humility and true power. Prayer does move God. Prayer and fasting moves both God and ourselves. I'm sure glad Queen Esther never subscribed to this teaching concerning fasting to be of no effect in moving God's heart. In a time of dire distress, she immediately called for a time of fasting as she sought God with no food or water for three days.

Years back I was in a meeting where I heard a preacher tell the audience, "Fasting is an act based out of fear, so it is pointless to fast; all we need to do is have faith." His polished message encouraged everyone to go out and have a huge meal after church and not worry about their problems. He made some good points in his sermon about faith and trust in God, but the overall message carried with it arrogance and pride that looked down upon prayer and fasting as something only done by those who were weak and incapable of delivering themselves.

The truth is that we can't deliver ourselves. We need God's help. Tragically, all this minister could do was preach a smooth message. There was not one miracle that took place in his meeting, not one sick person was healed, and no gifts of the Spirit were in operation. His misconceptions about prayer and fasting had left him in a position to preach an incomplete gospel, which is a gospel that has no demonstration of power. His pride had blinded him to how needy we all are in the Lord, and without Him we can do nothing. These are the ones who scoff at the old-school principles of fasting and fervent prayer even as they leisurely continue strolling down the path of religiosity. The whole time they have no clue of the Spirit's power to accomplish the most extraordinary feats.

I would like to share some Scriptures that verify examples of when God changed His heart toward a matter because of prayer, which thus altered events that appeared to be unchangeable.

In those days Hezekiah was sick and near death. And Isaiah the prophet, the son of Amoz, went to him and said to him, "Thus says the Lord: 'Set your house in order, for you shall die and not live.'" Then Hezekiah turned his face toward the wall, and prayed to the Lord, and said, "Remember now, O Lord, I pray, how I have walked before You in truth and with a loyal heart, and have done what is good in Your sight." And Hezekiah wept bitterly. And the word of the Lord came to Isaiah, saying, "Go and tell Hezekiah, 'Thus says the Lord, the God of David your father: I have heard your prayer, I have seen your tears; surely I will add to your days fifteen years'" (Isaiah 38:1-5).

We see that because Hezekiah prayed, humbled himself, and repented, God chose to reverse the previous word that was pronounced over him. This is a classic example that we can follow to also prevent tragedies such as divorce, bankruptcy, sickness, and other problems that often stem from a sin-related consequence. Hezekiah's main sin that got him into trouble was pride. It's important to realize that if we ever face dire situations in life, we should look to the Lord for help.

It says that Hezekiah "turned his face toward the wall." This phrase indicates that Hezekiah knew his only source of deliverance could come from the Lord. The doctors had tried their best and nothing had happened. His hope was no longer in doctors. Sometimes you are forced into a place where you must believe God for a miracle. In times of crisis you must turn your face toward the wall and refuse to look for natural help.

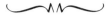

> The best of all medicines is resting and fasting. —
> Benjamin Franklin

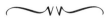

During times like these, a great inward battle will ensue between the spirit and soul. The soulish nature will want to panic. This is because the soul desperately wants a guarantee that something will work. The soul operates in the sense realm, wanting security through what can be seen or touched. Fasting and prayer with repentance will calm the soul and allow faith to arise to take hold of the promises of God. *Turn your face to the wall* and don't look to your rich uncle. Hang up the phone and stop sending emails to everyone under the sun. Don't expect to win a lottery ticket or try grasping at some wild possibility to fix your money problem, such as vainly hoping in a penny stock you may own to unexpectedly skyrocket overnight. Dismiss ideas of traveling to a rural village in Mexico to try some new type of experimental drug that is said to cure cancer. Instead, abandon yourself to God and trust in His Word. Quiet yourself and humbly go before God as Hezekiah did and you will see the Lord respond with the mercy, grace, and the sure deliverance that you need. The prophet Jonah also discovered that God can change His heart toward a matter when a sincere response is made and demonstrated through prayer and fasting.

> *Now the word of the Lord came to Jonah the second time, saying, "Arise, go to Nineveh, that great city, and preach to it the message that I tell you." So Jonah arose and went to Nineveh, according to the word of the Lord. Now Nineveh was an exceedingly great city, a three-day journey in extent. And Jonah began to enter the city on the first day's walk. Then he cried out and said, "Yet forty days, and Nineveh shall be overthrown!"*

> *So the people of Nineveh believed God, proclaimed a fast, and put on sackcloth, from the greatest to the least of them. Then word came to the king of Nineveh; and he arose from his throne and laid aside his robe, covered himself with sackcloth and sat in ashes. And he caused it to be proclaimed and published throughout Nineveh by the decree of the king and his nobles, saying, Let neither man nor beast, herd nor flock, taste anything; do not let them eat, or drink water. But let man and beast be covered with sackcloth, and cry mightily to God; yes, let every one turn from his evil way and from the violence that is in his hands. Who can tell if God will turn and relent, and turn away from His fierce anger, so that we may not perish? Then God saw their works, that they turned from their evil way; and God relented from the disaster that He had said He would bring upon them, and He did not do it* (Jonah 3:1-10).

The response from the king of Nineveh is amazing. The Assyrian empire was known as a kingdom that subdued other countries through brutality with no mercy, in order to expand their kingdom. It could well be that Jonah's initial resistance to going to Nineveh was because he carried a grudge against them for their reputation of committing so many atrocities. Jonah eventually agrees to deliver the prophetic word (after one very misguided boat trip) and the word strikes the people with great power. Can you imagine the sight?

A very godly prophet in India named Dr. D.G.S. Dhinakaran humbly told about being taken to Heaven in his frequent visions and shared what he saw on his amazing journeys. He described the time he meet the prophet Jonah while he was in Heaven. This is what Dr. Dhinakaran said:

> The Lord introduced me to a person of short stature and said, "This is Jonah and you can put forth your question to him." I was indeed surprised at the personality of this man as he looked very simple. Sure enough, I put the question to him, "Sir, how did you feel when you were in the belly of a big fish while you were in this world?" He smiled and said, "It was a very agonizing experience. The digestive acid in the belly of the fish would surround me from all sides. I would be submerged in that. The acid would try to digest me, my whole body would burn and I would scream at the top of my voice for God to help me to come out of its onslaught."
>
> He continued, "Then, most astonishingly, the 'grace of God' would come from another direction and surround me to redeem me from the power of that digestive acid. The grace of God would envelope me as an invisible fluid comforting and consoling, and with that the burning sensation would stop. I would be greatly relieved of

that agony and would have a great sigh of relief! However, after some time the whole scenario of crying out in agony would be repeated and again the grace of God would come forth to help me."[1]

Upon hearing the words of pending destruction spoken by Jonah, the king and all the people responded with deep repentance. Repentance is more than a word, it is something you do, and these people *did* repentance. Any real revival or repentance will often begin with faithful preaching and faithful hearing of God's Word, just as Jonah did in Nineveh. The people of Nineveh proclaimed a fast and put on sackcloth, from the greatest to the least of them, even down to the animals not eating or drinking. Sackcloth was a thick, coarse cloth normally made from goat's hair. Wearing sackcloth displayed a rejection of worldly comforts and pleasure in exchange for remorse and regret for sin. The people of Nineveh even repented on behalf of their animals, covering them with sackcloth as well. Because of the sincere change of heart, God spared Nineveh and pushed back the due judgment for 150 years.

Prayers of sincerity, coupled with energy, combined with humility and repentance, and expressed through fasting are able to greatly prevail in the eyes of God. It worked for Esther and the Jews. It even worked for the citizens of the pagan city of Nineveh who had no covenant relationship with God. It will also work for you, as God responds to your prayers in a specific and powerful way.

Endnote

1. D.G.S. Dhinakaran, *An Insight Into Heaven* (Mrs. Stella Dhinakaran, 2007).

CHAPTER FIVE

TOXIC CRISIS: UNDERSTANDING YOUR BODY WHILE FASTING

THE UNDERTAKING OF AN EXTENDED fast is something that is not to be done lightly. Personally, I would consider anything beyond ten days as an "extended" fast. To successfully accomplish an extended fast requires mental preparation for what lies ahead. A good understanding of what will take place with your body is very helpful so that the process is more bearable during the initial days of the fast, which is the most difficult time. When the Lord Jesus had His earthly ministry, we see examples of His everyday life. We see that He needed sleep and natural rest because He would become physically tired just as we do.

> *And a great windstorm arose, and the waves beat into the boat, so that it was already filling. But **He was in the stern, asleep on a pillow.** And they **awoke Him** and said to Him, "Teacher, do You not care that we are perishing?" **Then He arose** and*

rebuked the wind, and said to the sea, "Peace, be still!" And the wind ceased and there was a great calm (Mark 4:37-39).

*Now Jacob's well was there. Jesus therefore, **being wearied from His journey**, sat thus by the well. It was about the sixth hour* (John 4:6).

The four Gospels also share insights into the foods that Jesus ate, which are very different from the foods consumed by our modern-day North American culture. The following verses are a few examples. As you read them think of the differences in the types of food we eat and also how it is cooked and prepared as compared to Jesus and the twelve apostles with Him.

*Then He commanded the multitudes to sit down on the grass. And He took the **five loaves and the two fish**, and looking up to heaven, He blessed and broke and gave the loaves to the disciples; and the disciples gave to the multitudes. **So they all ate** and were filled, and they took up twelve baskets full of the fragments that remained (Matthew 14:19-20).*

*Now the next day, when they had come out from Bethany, He was hungry And seeing from afar a **fig tree** having leaves, **He went to see if perhaps He would find something on it…*** (Mark 11:12-13).

*Now it came to pass, as He sat at the table with them, that **He took bread**, blessed and broke it, and gave it to them. Then their eyes were opened and they knew Him; and He vanished from their sight (Luke 24:30-31).*

*But while they still did not believe for joy, and marveled, He said to them, "Have you any food here?" So they gave Him a piece of a **broiled fish and some honeycomb**. And **He took it and ate in their presence** (Luke 24:41-43).*

The above verses give us a small insight into the normal life of Jesus and His apostles. The foods they ate were what were grown locally in the region. They ate healthy foods that were fresh and natural. The world we live in today is very different. Often the fish we buy at the local supermarket has been raised in a fish farm in another country. Whether the fish farm is land-based or ocean-based, the fish usually live in cramped, filthy enclosures where they suffer from many types of disease and parasite infections. The parasites relentlessly attack the fish, causing them to develop large open sores and to lose their scales. The fish farmers lace the fish with powerful chemicals to fend off the parasites, but the chemicals are absorbed into the fish, creating high levels of toxicity which are passed on to the person who eats the fish.[1] Some fish that are kept in large net enclosures offshore escape the fish farm and swim away to affect healthy fish that live in the wild. When shopping at the grocery store, I endeavor to not buy fish unless it is caught in the wild, so it is free from the deformities, blindness, and toxin-laced problems of farm-raised fish. But when eating fish at restaurants, you may not be able to escape from being served farm-raised fish.

To lengthen thy life, lessen thy meals. —Benjamin Franklin

Much of the beef we eat today is a byproduct of cows that have been genetically enhanced. Today, anabolic steroids in the form of small time-release pellets are implanted in the cow's ears. The hormones slowly seep into the bloodstream, increasing hormone levels by two to five times. Some beef can contain excessive high concentrations of herbicides because the majority of all the herbicides used in the U.S. are sprayed on corn and soybeans, which are used primarily as feed for cattle. When consumed by cattle, the chemicals accumulate in their bodies and are passed on to consumers in finished cuts of beef. Beef ranks second only to tomatoes as the food posing the greatest cancer risk due to pesticide contamination. It ranks third of all foods in insecticide contamination.[2] I still eat beef, but I try to eat "good" beef that comes from cattle that have not been altered by modern science.

The list of challenges with the foods we eat goes on and on, whether it is excessive amounts of sugar or deliberate attempts by the food industry to insert high fructose corn syrup into almost everything we eat and drink. Recently I had lunch with a dear minister friend who is now in his late eighties. He went to the doctor for a check-up and was given a clean bill of health. While there he and the medical doctor had a discussion about the dangers of high fructose corn syrup. My minister friend said the doctor told him, "If high fructose corn syrup were removed from our drinks and foods, it would bankrupt the American medical industry." While I can't quote the doctor directly because I don't know who he is, I have no doubt to the truth of this statement.

When Jesus walked the earth during His earthly ministry, there were no sodas, no candy bars, no artificial sweeteners or food coloring dyes, no harmful preservatives to be concerned about, and none of the other modern-day toxins that are laced into so many of the foods we eat and the drinks we consume. There have been times when I have ministered in remote parts of the world where the western food culture had not yet invaded. I have seen men and women over seventy years of age who have never had a cavity in their life. Their teeth are brilliant white, perfectly straight, and clean despite having no toothbrushes, toothpaste, dental floss, or a dentist within several hundred miles! It's an amazing sight to see, but a sight that is quickly fading as the devil has done much to corrupt the global food supply.

Even still, God will bless the food we eat when we pray over it and sanctify it for His glory. Not everyone has the ability to shop at high-end health stores or drive to a large city where they can find gourmet specialty stores that cater to health-conscious eaters. This is why you should always pray over your food and ask God to bless it, so that whether it came from the sparkling clean waters of the deep blue Pacific Ocean or it was served at a restaurant that prides itself on farm-raised fish, you can eat in peace knowing that it is blessed by God. We should also pray over our food primarily with thanksgiving to God for His kind provision.

Many years ago while ministering in Uganda, we stayed at a very rural area where only the very basic necessities for living were supplied. There was no refrigeration and no hot running water. The meat we ate came from the butcher who displayed his cuts of beef out on an open table in the hot sun. Thousands of flies covered the raw meat. There was no understanding of germs, bacteria, or hygiene. The living conditions were rough, and you had to use your faith combined with common sense in order to not get sick.

Kelly and I stayed at what was considered to be a missionary outpost. Surrounding us were native grass huts made of clay mud for the walls, grass for the roof, and natural dirt floors. Each day we ate breakfast and dinner at the outpost. Our meals were the same type of food the locals ate. Eventually, a group of about 20 British students who were in their early 20s came and stayed here as well. Kelly and I sometimes talked with them after we would return from conducting our evangelistic meetings during the day. They were all nice and they sincerely loved the Lord, but I noticed on the first day they arrived that as they ate their meals they never prayed and thanked God for their food. This concerned me, and I actually spoke to some of them to sanctify their food with prayer because our stomachs were not developed to handle the food like the locals. I was concerned they would get sick. Each young person I spoke to told me it wasn't a problem. They said they didn't want to appear to be "religious" by being seen praying for their food. They said it was nothing to be concerned about.

Two days went by after their initial arrival, and every one of them got hit with a major case of food poisoning. Not one of them was able to get out of bed for five days because of being severely sick. They were so sick they would vomit in the bed and use the bathroom in the bed. Each one was burning up with fever. They all survived and were blessed just to be able to finally go home alive. Kelly and I ate the same food they did and drank from the same water source, but we never were the least bit sick, because we prayed over our food and asked God to bless it.

I must say in all seriousness that fasting when combined with a properly selected diet is the nearest approach to a "cure-all" that is possible to conceive—profoundly simple and simply profound! —John Tilden, M.D.

If Jesus prayed publicly for food to be blessed and Paul also prayed publicly for food to be blessed, then why should we be any different? We should always thank God the Father for our food. One of the joys of fasting is that it will give you a new appreciation for food. Everything tastes better after a fast. Fasting restores the joy of eating and increases our thankfulness to God for our meals.

> *Then He took the cup, and **gave thanks**, and said, "Take this and divide it among yourselves"* (Luke 22:17).

> *And when he had said these things, **he took bread and gave thanks to God in the presence of them all**; and when he had broken it he began to eat* (Acts 27:35).

When we fast, it helps to understand that the modern foods we have eaten have most likely carried some level of toxicity into our bodies. Many years ago, it was much easier and safer to go on a long water fast. With all of the food additives and potent prescription drugs which some people have to take for medical reasons, it is important that people who are highly toxic only fast under medical supervision. The fasting process will begin to flush the toxins from the body, but there can be some unpleasant side effects, especially during the first few days. Headaches, nausea, dizziness, and potential blackouts are common when starting off with a fast because these are side effects of the toxins being eliminated from your body.

Unfortunately, these same side effects often cause the person attempting the fast to stop due to a lack of knowledge of what is physiologically taking place, while not realizing that this is a message from the body trying to let them know that it needs to fast in order to be cleansed. Bad breath, weakness, hot and cold flashes, and the tongue turning yellow or white add to the discomfort which causes many people to snap and immediately call off the fast. What they fail to realize is that if they only get past the choppy waters of the first few days, then things begin to smooth out and become peaceful. This is why it is vital to take time to pray to receive God's strength in order to clear the initial hurdles of the negative side effects that are so often encountered during the first few days of fasting.

Fasting with only water is the most difficult fast, but also is the most effective in cleansing the body of toxins, removing impacted mucus from the bowels, burning up excessive fatty tissue, and cleansing deeply throughout the physical body. The luggage hauled into your body by the North American diet is packed up and hauled out of your house (body) and you are swept clean. When doing a fast with water, it normally takes 14 days for all toxins to be completely removed from your body. Usually after five days, the appetite for food has left and the strong initial side effects of toxic purging are also primarily behind you. The stomach and inner organs go into a restful "hibernation" while your body focuses one hundred percent on removing all remaining toxins stored deeply in the cells of fatty tissue. Fasting with water combined with prayer is also the fastest way to subdue the Adamic nature. It doesn't take long to see sinful passions and harmful addictions completely broken and the flesh kept in check. The realm of walking the crucified life is fully entered into, as the apostle Paul said:

> *I have been crucified with Christ*; *it is no longer I who live, but Christ lives in me; and the life which I now live in the flesh I live by faith in the Son of God, who loved me and gave Himself for me* (Galatians 2:20).

Fasting on water only is the ultimate experience in humility. Doing a water fast forces you to slow down. Becoming weak physically is now traded for the deluxe upgrade of clearly being more attuned to the Spirit of God. Things that normally seem to be of critical importance take a back seat to the overwhelming peace of God. Priorities are recalibrated and realigned. Even as your physical strength dissipates, the glory of God begins to increase in your life.

I desired as many as could to join together in fasting and prayer, that God would restore the spirit of love and of a sound mind to the poor deluded rebels in America. —John Wesley

Whether you have a fast or slow metabolism will also indicate what kind of energy level you can expect to have on a water fast. If you have a slow metabolism, then you will likely be more energetic during the fast. If you have a fast metabolism, like I do, then the first few days of a water fast can be a real energy crash. Most people who are naturally thin have less fat reserves to burn, so the first few days of an extended fast using only water can prove to be potentially a little more unpleasant. When I fast using only water, it's difficult for me to perform normal activities during the first few days of the fast. Because of this I make sure to keep my schedule as light as possible, including not driving. Driving during the initial days of on an extended fast is not wise, because your reaction time is greatly diminished. You may see that you are pulling up to a red light but the neurological message from your brain to your foot will be slower than normal, and your reaction time of putting your foot on the brake will be much, much slower than usual.

Once when I completed a three-day Esther-type fast with no food or water, I drove to the grocery store to get some vegetable juice. This was a mistake because every traffic light I came to would turn red and I had a challenging time getting my foot on the brake to stop in time. The Lord protected my driving, but I would not attempt it again when in this condition, nor would I recommend you doing so either.

The slow reaction is attributed to your blood being saturated with toxins, mucus, carcinogens, and other harmful effects that are getting flushed out through drinking lots of water. Your body will inwardly focus all of its attention on this assignment during a fast, so you don't want to do things that require quick responses. The key to successfully fasting with water is to drink lots of water, preferably distilled water or spring water, which will speed up the detoxification process, and spend as much time in prayer as possible.

Juice fasting is also an excellent way to seek God in fasting and prayer. It is a great alternative to water fasting because the juice will provide healthy energy, making it possible to work a full day even when fasting. When juice fasting I highly recommend you only use freshly-derived juice. If you use bottled or canned juice that comes from the grocery store shelves, then it does not have the fresh, life-giving vitamins and minerals that carry the tremendous healing ability like fresh-squeezed juice does. When you use freshly prepared juice, then your hunger for food will also go away between four to five days. If you don't use freshly prepared juice, then your hunger for food will continue to stay with you!

Without mortifying the taste, it is impossible to preserve innocence, since it was by the indulgence of his appetite that Adam fell. —Saint Catharine of Sipenna

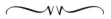

I first learned this many years back on a 40-day juice fast using apple juice. The apple juice I purchased was from the grocery store and was not fresh. Because of this I suffered the mental anguish of my appetite never leaving even up to the final, fortieth day. While the overall fast was highly productive, the constant appetite proved to be a real distraction. The Lord gave me wonderful supernatural experiences and visions during the day, but I also had constant dreams of doughnuts, milkshakes, and pizza while I slept at night! Once I made the discovery of only using fresh juice, I've made sure to never repeat that old mistake again.

Fasting with juice eliminates the "toxic shock" often associated with a water-only fast. However, it takes a longer time for a juice fast to flush your body completely clean from toxins, usually about 30 days. Many European sanitariums recommend juice fasting for their patients who suffer from a wide variety of diseases. In my studies I have noticed that most European sanitariums recommend their patients to juice fast for 30 days to solve difficult health problems, while under medical supervision.[3]

Fresh juice supplies ample energy even though you will still lose quite a bit of weight on an extended juice fast. The key is to drink often and enjoy the deep peace of God that will begin to flood into your life. Take the extra time to pray and enjoy trying different fruit juice combinations. Be careful not to use too much orange juice, because it is highly acidic which becomes very noticeable after five days of fasting. Apple and carrot juice are great when mixed together. The combinations are endless when making freshly prepared juice. When juicing, try to eliminate as much pulp as possible and keep the juice thin, or else the pulp will need to be digested, which reawakens your stomach, which then causes a return of your appetite.

While you are on your fast, make sure you bathe daily because many of the toxins will be released through the pores of your skin. When you brush your teeth, also gently scrub your tongue where many of the toxins are also dispelled from your body. Be mindful that you will have bad breath until the toxins have departed, but I would not suggest chewing gum because the sugar in the gum is strong enough to awaken your stomach's digestive system. A good mouthwash should be used regularly to keep your breath fresh, but use extra caution not to swallow any of the mouthwash because it would cause great shock to an empty stomach.

Any search on the Internet about fasting will bring up the subject of using enemas. On all the fasts that I have done, I've never used enemas and I don't recommend you use them either. An enema is the injection of a liquid into the rectum for the purpose of cleansing out the bowels. Some doctors have concluded that enemas can impair normal bowel function and slow down recovery of the bowels once an extended fast is completed. Using an enema to cleanse the bowels before starting a fast, in my opinion, runs against the laws of nature. I agree with Dr. Herbert M. Shelton who made the following quote:

> Fasting animals do not employ enemas nor anything that may be regarded as serving the same purpose. Fasting seals and salmon, hibernating bears and snakes, fasting sick and wounded animals, regardless of the length of their fasts, employ no measures to force bowel action. Since this thing has been tried out on the plane of instinct for unnumbered thousands of years, and has been approved by nature, we need have no fear of fasting without the employment of enemas.[4]

Sometimes people suggest that when doing a fast you should supplement your body with protein to keep from losing muscle.

God designed our bodies in a remarkable way so that when we fast, our bodies keep protein stored away in the healthy tissues of our body. There have been people who actually died when only consuming a liquid protein diet and eating no food for excessive durations. Essentially they were doing a water fast with a liquid protein supplement for as long as three months. These extreme fads proved to be unhealthy and at times deadly.

You can take liquid protein supplementation on a juice fast, but it's not advisable on a lengthy water fast. Only during starvation does the body strip protein from healthy tissue in order to survive. On a 30-day water fast, a person will normally lose just one to two pounds of muscle mass. So you can see that God has designed our bodies to be extremely efficient in burning up the nonessential fat tissues, tumors, degenerative tissues, viruses, bacteria, and any other type of "junk" that can be used for fuel, while essentially storing protein for survival situations related to starvation.

It is wise to seek proper professional guidance when fasting, especially if you are on prescription medication. Recently I spoke at a great church during one of my many ministry travels. The pastor was very gracious and kind and we had outstanding meetings while I was there. One evening after the service had concluded we went to dinner and were talking about unusual supernatural experiences. This pastor told me his story about when he did a water fast the previous year and got into trouble. He was taking a very strong prescription drug every day and he did not tell his doctor he was fasting. On the tenth day he was in his house drinking a glass of water in the kitchen. Suddenly he blacked out and fell completely forward, sriking his jaw against the granite kitchen countertop on the way down, and lay passed out on the floor.

He was soon discovered by another family member who called the ambulance. He was rushed to the hospital where the medical team went to work reviving him. This pastor told me that the head doctor later personally informed him that he had died three times, but he was brought back each time and the third time he pulled through to live. When the doctor found out the pastor had fasted while on a very strong prescription drug, he became very upset and reproved him for doing this because it directly affected his heart and caused it to stop. The pastor was completely unaware of the potential medical problems that were lurking. His desire to fast and pray was sincere, but we must use wisdom in all we do.

The pastor continued to tell me that he recovered quickly, and after a week he returned to his church to preach. As he was preaching his two front teeth fell out right in the middle of his message! They had been knocked loose from when he previously hit his jaw on the countertop. The church members were shocked, but he kept right on preaching while a deacon handed him some tissues to wipe away the blood. I'll tell you one thing—that man of God took every obstacle in stride that showed up in his path. He didn't let anything slow him down or deter him from going on with the Lord. He eventually went to the dentist and had the two front teeth replaced.

Understanding some of the basic physiological reactions to fasting will help you push off from shore and get over the first initial waves of discomfort without quitting prematurely. Prepare your mind before going into your fast. Usually I will enjoy a nice meal out with my family and spend the day doing whatever my wife and daughter want to do, giving extra attention to them because during the fast I will be in more of a "retreat" mode in order to focus on prayer. After a good pizza and some tiramisu, the last thing I often eat is about five ounces of dried plums (prunes) to get a little extra fiber in order to avoid any potential constipation. Once into the fast, the bowels will go into "hibernation" and have a nice rest for a while.

When this is accomplished, I now step mentally over into my spiritual boat and push off from shore, trusting to be carried by the Spirit of God to my destination of deep communion with God and entering into fervent prayer. This journey awaits you as well. Let the Holy Spirit speak to your heart now. Let the wind of God fill your sails as you venture into the heart of the Father through fasting and prayer.

Endnotes

1. Tara Lohan, "How Farm-Raised Salmon Are Turning Our Oceans Into Dangerous and Polluted Feedlots," AlterNet, September 2, 2009, accessed January 17, 2012, http://www.alternet.org/water/142270/how_farm-raised_salmon_are_turning_our_oceans_into_dangerous_and_polluted_feedlots_/.

2. Food First, "Beyond Beef," McSpotlight, Background: Health, accessed October 02, 2011, http://www.mcspotlight.org/media/reports/beyond.html.

3. "Therapeutic Fasting Worldwide Links," SCI, accessed January 17, 2012, http://sci.pam.szczecin.pl/~fasting/. (This is a link page with world-wide fasting centers.)

4. Herbert M. Shelton, *The Hygienic System: Fasting and Sun Bathing* (Whitefish, MT: Literary Licensing, LLC, 2011).

CHAPTER SIX

DON'T DOUBT THE LORD

THERE'S SOMETHING FASCINATING ABOUT THE Lord—because He loves us so much He will always be truthful with us, even when it means He has to correct us. During His earthly ministry, it was very clear that the Lord loved the twelve apostles. Yet, when they at times would drift into unbelief, the Lord was quick and firm to correct them. We even see this after His resurrection, when He appears to the apostles as they were hiding in a room with the doors securely shut and feeling discouraged.

> *Later He appeared to the eleven as they sat at the table; and* **He rebuked their unbelief** *and hardness of heart, because they did not believe those who had seen Him after He had risen* (Mark 16:14).

When Jesus greeted the apostles after His resurrection the first thing He said to them was, *"Peace be with you"* (John 20:19). The apostles were overwhelmed with relief to see the Lord, and the Lord was very happy to see them again. But the Lord does not sweep problems underneath the carpet and intentionally avoid situations that need to be addressed. After His kind greeting and miraculous appearance, He got right to the point of rebuking them for their unbelief and hardness of heart. The Lord Jesus is very kind and compassionate, but whatever trial you may be going through, He still expects you to believe His Word and not doubt Him. He does not make exceptions to this or play personal favorites with anybody.

One of the great benefits of fasting and prayer is that it causes your faith to soar. Whereas before you may have known in your heart that you lacked the genuine faith to believe for a miracle, you now are enabled to grab a hold of it by an unshakable faith. Your faith becomes focused like a laser beam and there is a deep knowing that you will see your prayer answered. We also see the role of productive faith clearly demonstrated through Jesus when he cast out a deaf and dumb spirit from a young boy.

*Then they brought him to Him. And when he saw Him, immediately the spirit convulsed him, and he fell on the ground and wallowed, foaming at the mouth. So He asked his father, "How long has this been happening to him?" And he said, "From childhood. And often he has thrown him both into the fire and into the water to destroy him. But if You can do anything, have compassion on us and help us." Jesus said to him, "If you can believe, all things are possible to him who believes." Immediately the father of the child cried out and said with tears, "Lord, I believe; help my unbelief!" When Jesus saw that the people came running together, He rebuked the unclean spirit, saying to it, "Deaf and dumb spirit, I command you, come out of him and enter him no more!" Then the spirit cried out, convulsed him greatly, and came out of him. And he became as one dead, so that many said, "He is dead." But Jesus took him by the hand and lifted him up, and he arose. And when He had come into the house, His disciples asked Him privately, "Why could we not cast it out?" So He said to them, "**This kind can come out by nothing but prayer and fasting**"* (Mark 9:20-29).

The problem which the apostles had was not with the evil spirit. The root of the problem was their lack of faith to remove the evil spirit. A lack of faith produces unbelief, which in turn creates an atmosphere of doubt, which produces zero results. The apostles asked Jesus in private why they could not cast the evil spirit out. I'm confident the reason they asked in private was because they were publicly embarrassed by their failure to deliver the child from the evil spirit. The classic answer that Jesus gave still rings true today. *"This kind can come out by nothing but prayer and fasting."* Fasting and prayer cures unbelief. That which previously seemed to be impossible now comes within reach for you to perceive and accomplish.

When I got to town to start a revival a lady contacted me who ran a boarding house. She said, "Brother Finney, do you know a Father Nash? He and two other men have been at my boarding house for the last three days, but they haven't eaten a bite of food. I opened the door and peeped in at them because I could hear them groaning, and I saw them down on their faces. They have been this way for three days, lying prostrate on the floor and groaning. I thought something awful must have happened to them. I was afraid to go in and I didn't know what to do. Would you please come see about them?"

"No it isn't necessary," I replied. "They just have a spirit of travail in prayer." —Charles Finney

Once I had an experience where the Lord revealed to me the importance of not doubting Him in regards to having my needs met. Even while I was ministering regularly and traveling often to speak in meetings, my bills had begun to accumulate. The economy had taken a great shaking, causing many Americans to lose their jobs. Our regular support that normally comes in from our ministry partners fell dramatically as many lost their jobs and had to scramble to find new work, often in a totally different career field. The offerings in the meetings in which I spoke were also considerably lower than before, due also to the economic downturn. This left me struggling to pay ministry and personal bills. I began to spend extra time in prayer to seek the Lord's help in this situation. After much prayer, the Lord spoke to me the following verse. It came to me as I just happened to open my Bible to the book of Isaiah, and this verse lifted off the page and appeared to hover in the air like a 3D effect.

> *Fear not, for I am with you; be not dismayed, for I am your God. I will strengthen you, yes, I will help you, I will uphold you with My righteous right hand* (Isaiah 41:10).

Receiving this verse brought much peace to my heart. I have learned over the years that whenever the Holy Spirit quickens a verse like that to me, than it's the same thing as Jesus appearing in person and speaking it to me. For the next few days I rejoiced at having heard from the Lord, but nothing changed in the natural. A few more days went by and the bills continued to get further behind. The pressure began to mount. What was I to do? To pile further difficulty on top of the situation I had to face going on an extended international trip within two weeks. The last thing I wanted to do was leave home with the bills unpaid. As the pressure grew I began to let thoughts slip into my heart, doubting whether or not God was going to help me. Even after having had the experience of the verse rising from the page of my Bible, I had now begun to struggle with trusting God. A great trial had come upon me and my faith was wavering. I felt like Peter who briefly took his eyes off of the Lord while walking on the water and began to sink.

That evening I went down to the office to pray. While trying to pray but finding myself mainly remonstrating about my situation, the office phone rang. It was Kelly calling from home. She needed to update me on some bills that were reaching a critical stage of needing to be taken care of immediately. Her voice was calm as she informed me which ones were most urgent. My wife is the greatest administrator I have ever met; she always keeps things in perfect order and does a tremendous job of orchestrating the many activities of the ministry. As she was talking to me, someone walked into the room although the doors to the office were locked. The person stood behind my left shoulder waiting for me to complete my phone call. I told Kelly, "I've got to go, and I've got to go now."

She said, "Is everything OK?"

"Yes," I replied, "I will explain it later."

As I hung up the phone and slowly turned around, I already knew who my visitor was. Turning to my side my spiritual eyes became opened and there I saw the Lord Jesus. He stood waiting for me and He was not smiling. With a serious tone He said, "We've got to get to the bottom of this."

Having said those words, we began to go down. The best way I can describe what happened was like getting in an elevator and going down from a great height. The Lord went with me. We were traveling in the elevator of my heart, descending toward the lower depths of my spirit. As we descended, I saw for the first time the gigantic spiritual expanse within me. It reminded me somewhat of a time when I visited Carlsbad Caverns in New Mexico. When I saw the caves for the first time as a young boy, I was amazed at the enormous size. Yet my spirit, my inward man, was not dark like a cave but illuminated by the indwelling Holy Spirit. I had no idea my spirit was so large on the inside!

We continued to descend quickly and soon approached the very core of my being. This was where the real Steven Brooks could be found, in the truest sense. As we reached the bottom floor I stepped off of the spiritual elevator onto a solid rock foundation. There was no lower level to descend to; I had gone all the way to the very bottom. Simultaneously, in this vision I could also see the floor in my office while sitting in my chair. It was as if the Lord had given me x-ray vision and I could see right through the carpet and to the concrete foundation beneath. I now stood with the Lord on the bedrock of my spirit, the ocean floor of my heart.

As we stood there, the Lord looked at me intensely but lovingly, and said, "What are you going to do about this?" When He said that, a large billboard sign floated up before us with the following words written in large oversized letters: *Though He slay me, yet will I trust in Him.*

I read the sign and then looked at the Lord. This was a verse I had read somewhere before in the Bible, but I couldn't at the moment remember where it was from. With desperation I wanted to answer the Lord's question. In my heart I knew I had allowed doubt and unbelief to creep in and choke the word which God spoke to me earlier from Isaiah 41:10. Before I could answer, the Lord preempted me and said, "Don't answer now; think about it first." The Lord then departed and the vision lifted.

Saint Francis of Assisi devoured fasting as a man devours food. —G.K. Chesterton

For the next three days I pondered what the Lord had said to me. It didn't take me long to find the statement on the sign, which was taken from Job 13:15. It's so easy for many Christians to say, "Lord, I trust you," but not really have a clue as to what that actually means. The Lord was taking me to a new level. He was stretching me beyond my current spiritual experience. My theology was being upended and expanded in a rapid way. I was determined to let the Lord lead me even though nothing was making sense and my financial situation was continuing to appear to go downhill. In my heart, I made a fresh commitment personally that I would give it all to Him—that I would trust anything He told me to do and not doubt Him. A greater measure of faith began to fill my heart and I knew everything was going to be all right. However, I wanted to somehow express to the Lord my answer to His question, "What are you going to do about this?"

After three days of prayer and reflective meditation on what the Lord shared with me, I felt in my heart that I was now ready to answer Him. The Holy Spirit led me to not respond until there was an anointing to respond. I told Kelly that I was going to go back down to the office and pray throughout the night. At about 5:00 p.m., I reached the office and began to pray. For the next four hours I walked around the inside of the office and prayed in tongues. There wasn't any unusual anointing or manifestation until about 9:00 p.m.

At 9:00 p.m., I noticed for the first time that as I walked around the room there was a certain spot that, when I walked through it, there was an awareness of having walked through a beam of heavenly light that was shining down. I said to myself, "Wow, that sure was nice. I wonder if it will happen again?" Slowly, I walked around the room and without stopping I again walked through that same spot. As I did it felt like a warm, soft heavenly light shone all around me and upon me. I did not stop but kept moving forward at a slow walk as I circled the room again. This time I said to myself, "If that happens again the next time I walk by that spot, then I'm going to talk to the Lord and answer His question."

As I came around the room for the third time and stepped into that illuminated place, a tremendous wave of light and glory came over me and flooded my soul. I dropped to my knees and began to praise and worship God with everything I had. Tears began to stream down my face, and I cried great tears of relief as I told the Lord how much He meant to me, and that I was sorry that I ever doubted Him. I said, "Lord, even if You slay me, yet will I trust You. Even if I don't have anything in this world, yet will I trust you and praise You. With all of my heart I worship and adore You, and I submit to Your loving and kind hand, for I know You only have my best interest at heart." Oh, the glory! Oh, the inexpressible joy that filled my heart. It was pure spiritual ecstasy, beyond my ability to describe in words. When it was all over I felt totally spent and undone. I went to sleep that night on the office floor in total bliss, knowing that God was in complete control of my life, and that nothing could take me out of His hand.

Within one month after this experience we had the largest offering come into the ministry that we had ever received. During that month other large offerings came in from people I didn't even know from foreign countries around the world and in the United States. Every unpaid bill was wiped out and our storehouses were filled up. We were greatly refreshed and uplifted. Through this experience and others I have learned to never doubt the Lord.

It doesn't matter how big and intimidating your problem is, the Lord can crush any problem and give you the strength to walk in victory. Jesus has never lost a fight; He's the Champion. Have you been hearing negative news and negative prophecies lately? Would you like some good news? Well, here is some really good news:

> *...When the enemy shall come in like a flood, the Spirit of the Lord shall lift up a standard against him* (Isaiah 59:19 KJV).

Prophetic Word to the Reader

> *"You may feel like you are on the ropes, but help is on the way. God is going to subdue your enemies before you. The knock-out punch to your enemy is now being delivered by the Spirit of God. The anointing removes the burdens from your life, and the yoke around your neck is crushed to dust and blown away with the wind. Pray in the Spirit and give God praise for your victory, for surely this day is one in which you will go forward, unhindered by the things of the past. The very same God who delivered Moses, David, Daniel, Naomi, and many others is rescuing you now. Bless His holy name! Bless the name of the Lord! For the Lord is great, and greatly to be praised. Lift up to the Lord your highest praise, for as you do the Lord is sending, sending, yes sending His mighty angels of deliverance to make a way for you. Shout out His praise, for the battle is the Lord's, and He has won the victory for you."*

CHAPTER SEVEN

REVELATION KNOWLEDGE RELEASED THROUGH PRAYER AND FASTING

ONCE I WENT TO MINISTER IN a church in California. Leaving from North Carolina, I flew westward along with Kelly and my daughter Abigail. With a two-hour drive just to get to the airport, then a four and a half hour flight plus two layovers, with each stop having two hours of sitting in an airport, it was a full day of travel. We reached our destination at 1:00 in the morning and were looking forward to getting some rest; needless to say, we were exhausted. The host pastor picked us up at the airport and drove us to the hotel he had arranged for us. Normally we inquire about the hotel when we preplan the meeting with the host pastor. He had previously reassured us over the phone that he had a very nice hotel picked out for us. Since those days I have learned to be more inquisitive about the hotel in which I will be staying. Not everyone has the same idea of what is a good and acceptable hotel.

By the time we arrived at the hotel with our luggage, it was 1:30 in the morning. When we pulled up to the hotel we were shocked to see an old, run-down motel with broken glass in some of the windows (some windows had no glass, just the wind blowing in!), suspicious characters hanging around who looked like gang members, and a host of other negative features that made me think I had somehow been translated to a war-torn, third-world country. But this was America, and there was unfortunately a breakdown in communication with the pastor as to what was a good hotel.

We were so tired that Kelly and I thought it best to not mention our disappointment to the pastor. The pastor stayed with us as we checked in and gave us our room keys and then left. We walked to our room; I opened the door and turned on the lights and saw that there were large black spiders on the wall! After I killed the spiders, we got into our sleeping clothes. I pulled back the comforter blanket on the bed and to my shock saw that the sheets had blood on them! Whew! This motel wasn't going to earn a five-star rating with me. We took off the blood-stained sheets and slept without any covering.

Despite our enduring unpleasant treatment from the host pastor, we went to sleep with hearts that chose to overlook a fault and cover it with the blood of Jesus. That night, in that run-down, dumpy motel, the Lord Jesus came and visited me. I had not been asleep long. I was awoken somehow and sat straight up in bed. When I looked at the clock it said 4:30 a.m. I noticed my wife and daughter were sleeping soundly as the Lord appeared to me while reaching out His hand and inviting me to come with Him. He lifted me up and walked with me as we stepped into a large book that in appearance was the size of a house. It was the Book of James. Some of the most amazing heavenly experiences and visitations from the Lord have happened to me in the most humbling of places. The Lord often does this to offset discouraging difficulties and trials that come our way. The greater the hardships we endure for Him, the greater is our revelation and understanding of Him. I would rather stay in a rundown motel and have a visitation from Jesus than stay in a five-star hotel and be without His presence.

> Prayer is reaching out and after the unseen; fasting, letting go of all that is seen and temporal. Fasting helps express, deepens, confirms the resolution that we are ready to sacrifice anything, even ourselves, to attain what we seek for the kingdom of God. —Andrew Murray

Just weeks before this trip to California, I was in a ministry conference and saw a prophet friend of mine. We were both speaking at the same conference, but had not seen each other for almost a year. He was the first speaker and was preaching when he noticed me sitting on the front row. He stopped and publicly said, "It sure is nice to see James sitting on the front row." The large audience immediately laughed and spoke in unison, "His name is Steven." My friend was so embarrassed. He said, "I don't know why I did that, Steven and I have known each other for years!" There are prophetic slip-ups that are intentional by the Holy Spirit; be aware of such spiritual precursors that foreshadow coming events.

When I went into the Book of James, I not only saw the Word in greater revelation, but it was experiential as well. In other words, I heard and felt what the Holy Spirit was conveying through James when this was originally written. The Lord took extra time to share with me about a very strong statement that James made to particular members of the church. He said:

Adulterers and adulteresses! Do you not know that friendship with the world is enmity [hatred, hostility] with God? (James 4:4)

> If you say I will fast when God lays it on me, you never will. You are too cold and indifferent. Take the yoke upon you. —Dwight L. Moody

There are many in the church today who are cheating on the Lord. With their lips they acknowledge that they love God, but their actions expose them as ones who have cheating hearts. These are the type of Christians who try to be good so they won't go to hell, but they still love the world and don't want to give up certain base passions that have the seat of priority within their hearts. James actually called these types of Christians "adulterers." When was the last time you heard a pastor in an American church actually stand before his or her congregation and publicly confront those who were committing a form of spiritual adultery? I'm all for messages that motivate and encourage, but we should preach the whole counsel of the Word of God.

For I have not shunned to declare to you the whole counsel of God (Acts 20:27).

Paul did not just teach one type of message. He shared the whole counsel of God. Today, the western church preaches

126

messages that are primarily centered on positive, motivational topics that are designed to make people feel better about themselves. But there is a major disconnect for many Christians because it is obvious that there is still a lack of God's blessing resting upon their lives. This is because God cannot bless disobedience.

Under the Old Covenant, when the nation of Israel walked according to God's laws and commandments, they were blessed. When they committed spiritual adultery and their hearts turned to worship other gods, they would eventually suffer the consequences of their sin, and their once-blessed lives would begin to disintegrate. This is why James spoke of the frustration of Christians whose prayers are not answered and why things never work out right for these type of people. It is because of their misguided priorities and their cheating hearts that are full of the lusts of the world. When the Lord took me into verse five, my heart became overwhelmed with the heartbeat of God.

Or do you think that the Scripture says in vain, "The Spirit who dwells in us yearns jealously"? (James 4:5)

It was at this time that the Lord allowed me to feel the constant betrayal and rejection that happens to Him daily when His people cheat on Him by flirting with the world and then allowing themselves to be seduced by a corrupt, broken world system that is opposed to God and all that He represents. I was reminded of Asa who was a former king of Judah. When Asa was loyal to the Lord, he saw amazing miracles. Once, Zerah the Ethiopian came against Judah with an army of one million men! In response, Asa went to the Lord and prayed one of the most powerful, faith-filled prayers I've ever heard. He said:

...Lord, it is nothing for you to help, whether with many or with those who have no power; help us, O Lord our God, for we rest on You, and in Your name we go against this multitude.

O Lord, You are our God; do not let man prevail against You!
(2 Chronicles 14:11)

The response to this prayer was breathtaking. The Ethiopians were overthrown and broken before the Lord and His army. Oh, the potential that Asa had. God began to work so strongly through him. But then came a betrayal. Later on, when faced with a possible attack from a much smaller army from the northern kingdom of Israel, Asa did not consult the Lord but hired an army from Syria to fight on his behalf. This deeply grieved the Lord's heart. God sent a prophet to King Asa, saying:

> *...Because you have relied on the king of Syria, and have not relied on the Lord your God, therefore the army of the king of Syria has escaped from your hand. Were the Ethiopians and the Lubim not a huge army with very many chariots and horsemen? Yet, because you relied on the Lord, He delivered them into your hand. For the eyes of the Lord run to and fro throughout the whole earth, to show Himself strong on behalf of those **whose heart is loyal** to Him* (2 Chronicles 16:7-9).

We need to have loyal hearts. The Holy Spirit who lives in us is very jealous about our marriage covenant with the Lord. After feeling the Lord's heart and the painful betrayals He at times goes through, I reached a point where I thought my heart was going to explode. Flashes of anger and deep pains of rejection all shot through my heart while being magnified many times over because of the number of believers who daily cheat on Him. Just when I thought I couldn't take it anymore, the Lord took me out of the Book. I've read the book of James many times, but I never had any idea how deeply possessive and jealous God is toward us. I for one do not ever want to provoke Him. I love how The Message Bible translates James 4:5.

> *You're cheating on God. If all you want is your own way, flirting with the world every chance you get, you end up enemies of*

God and His way. And do you suppose God doesn't care? The proverb has it that "He's a fiercely jealous lover." And what He gives in love is far better than anything else you will find (James 4:5 MSG).

Fasting is a good way to break the love affair with the world and turn your eyes back onto the Lord. Once when ministering in a certain city in California, a nice brother in his late twenties told me how God had blessed him with a good job. With the extra income he was able to go out and buy a large-screen, high-definition television that he could mount on his living room wall. The problem, he said, was that he did not have the willpower to stop watching his television. He confessed to me that every day after work he went home and watched six hours of sports on cable television. His fleshly nature was controlling his life, and he had become spiritually dry—and he was the praise and worship leader in the church. The solution he needed was not to throw the television in the trash, but rather to fast and pray and reestablish God's priorities. I encouraged him to fast and pray, and also suggested he turn off the television for at least two weeks. The Lord does not initiate intimacy; it is our responsibility to seek Him and not let anything interfere with having the Lord as number one in our hearts.

Draw near to God and He will draw near to you... (James 4:8).

In the vision at the motel, after I came out of the Book of James the Lord personally talked with me about my ministry. He encouraged me to be steadfast in preaching His Word and in praying for the sick. He also spoke to me about some personal things which were a great blessing to have insight on.

As we walk with hearts that are fully knitted to the Lord, we will often have experiences that will take us beyond mental knowledge into advanced learning gained by the Holy Spirit illuminating our spiritual eyes. Once the Lord also took me into the Book of Second Corinthians. It was wonderful; I saw and learned more in twenty minutes then I had in years of study. These particular types of experiences have been ongoing throughout church history.

A dear friend of mine, Wade Taylor, wrote a book called *Secret of the Stairs*. Wade had just graduated from Bible college in 1959 when he was sitting around with the other college students relaxing one late afternoon. As they talked, all of the students decided to go out and see the evening movie except for Wade. He thought it would be more productive to use his time to pray and read God's Word. He shared with me how he went back to his room and opened his Bible to the Song of Solomon. What happened next was something he did not expect. He was taken into the book!

He saw the main characters—the bride, the bridegroom, and the daughters of Jerusalem. He felt the passion of the groom toward his bride and saw clearly the relationship between this beautiful book and Christ's relationship with His Church. Through this enlightened condition, he was anointed to write *Secret of the Stairs*, a devotional book that has inspired many to more deeply pursue the Lord.

Wade also shared with me how the mystic saint John Wright Follette also regularly experienced being taken into the Word of God to partake of fresh manna. The writings of Follette certainly reflect knowledge that is not gleaned through academic studies, but through intimate communion with God. Wade was greatly influenced by John Wright Follette and had a close relationship with him. Follette laid his hands upon Wade to receive his mantle to teach and impart the qualities of the spiritual life. Many years later, it was Wade Taylor who laid hands on me and prayed for his mantle and the mantle he received from John Wright Follette to be imparted into my life and ministry.

> Bear up the hands that hang down, by faith and prayer, support the tottering knees. Have you any days of fasting and prayer? Storm the Throne of Grace and persevere therein, and mercy will come down. —John Wesley

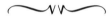

As we put the Lord first in our lives and fast often and pray to keep Him is His rightful place as Lord, we will begin to see the fruitful results that come from living a life of holiness and obedience. Let us be honest and sincere in our walk with God and make the necessary changes in order to walk in revival power. Let us cleanse ourselves from all that would defile and draw near with hearts assured of our completeness in Him. By doing so, we position ourselves to live in all the privileges and blessings that God intends for us to experience.

CHAPTER EIGHT

THE ART OF WAITING ON THE LORD

THERE ARE DIFFERENT TYPES OF prayer and there are different levels of prayer. Often you reach moments in your prayer time when you sense you have covered all of your bases. There comes a satisfaction in knowing through the inward witness that your heart is full of peace and that your prayers are being effective. It is during times like these when we can conclude our times of prayer and enter into the activities of the day, or if time allows we can continue to wait on the Lord in a prayerful attitude. Waiting on the Lord is not actually prayer. Waiting denotes the art of staying still with the intent of hearing from God should He decide He would like to share something. There are three types of waiting that are mentioned in Scripture. They are waiting *on* the Lord, waiting *for* the Lord, and waiting *with* the Lord. They each are similar to one another but yet retain their own distinctive flavor.

Most believers are familiar with the well-known passage from Isaiah that talks about waiting on the Lord and having your strength renewed like the eagle. This passage is the introductory verse that opens up the secret world of going beyond prayer that is based on requests, petitions, and asking, and moving into a deep relationship with God that is constant and continually unfolding. There is nothing wrong with asking God for things. We are even instructed to ask so that we might receive so that our joy may be full. There is a place for petition and presentation of our needs and desires. It is a blessing to be able to come boldly before the throne of grace and *ask* for help in our time of need. But again, waiting on the Lord is technically not the same as prayer. Consider the following verse.

> *Have you not known? Have you not heard? The everlasting God, the Lord, the Creator of the ends of the earth, neither faints nor is weary. His understanding is unsearchable. He gives power to the weak, and to those who have no might He increases strength. Even the youths shall faint and be weary, and the young men shall utterly fall,* **but those who wait on the Lord** *shall renew their strength; they shall mount up with wings like eagles, they shall run and not be weary, they shall walk and not faint (Isaiah 40:28-31).*

Waiting on the Lord is, in essence, ministering to the Lord. It is a time when we sit calmly in the Lord's Presence, enjoying His companionship and being quiet. It's like marriage in some ways. Married couples sometimes enjoy just sitting together with a good cup of coffee and looking at a sunset. There is not a need to say anything, but rather a satisfaction and peace of simply being together. The Hebrew word for "wait" used in this passage of Scripture by Isaiah means to "long for and look for with expectancy." This is a deep realm of fellowship with God. When you wait on the Lord, you approach God not because of a need, but rather to be with Him just because He is so wonderful. How many believers today spend time with God with no other desire than only to be with Him? How would you feel as a husband if the only time your wife spoke to you was to ask you for a new dress or a bigger house? What would a father think if his young son only talked to him when he wanted a new video game or a better skateboard? There's nothing wrong with asking, but if this represents the majority of the times there is spoken communication, then there will be a gap in the relationship because the conversation is constantly lopsided.

In regard to my own experience, I will say that unless I had the spirit of prayer I could do nothing. If I lost the spirit of grace and supplication even for a day or an hour I found myself unable to preach with power and efficiency, or to win souls by personal conversation. —Charles Finney

There have been times after I have already prayed when I will come back later in the day before the Lord to wait on Him. I am not there to pray; I have already prayed at an earlier time. With my voice I will say to the Lord, "Lord Jesus, I am not here to ask You for anything. I am only here to spend time with You. If you would like to share something with me, then that is fine. If You do not want to speak anything specifically to me, then that is fine as well. My purpose for being here is to wait on You because I enjoy being in Your Presence." Out of these times of waiting, I have had experiences happen that I would not trade for anything. Sometimes I've waited hours and not one thing would happen as far as experiencing some type of supernatural activity. At times like this, your intellectual brain will tell you that you are wasting your time. But eventually the brain (intellect) becomes calm and your spiritual ears become super keen. Don't ever think for a moment that God is not aware of you seeking Him.

As you wait on the Lord, an unusual quickening by the Spirit of God begins to take place. Several months ago I was at my home while my wife and daughter were gone out of town. On the day they were to arrive home, I decided to spend that entire day with the Lord. Kelly told me the night before that she would not reach home until the next day at 5:00 p.m. On that day, I awoke early in the morning and spent several hours in diligent prayer. Once my prayer time was complete, I felt very refreshed. It was then I said, "Lord Jesus, I am through praying and I thank You that You hear and answer my prayers. Now I have the whole day free, and I want to spend it waiting on You. If You would like to speak to me, then I'm listening with anticipation. I'm here to wait on You with expectancy."

All that day I spent with the Lord shut up in the room. I started waiting at 9:00 a.m. and didn't go anywhere. At times I would sing songs to the Lord. The day began to pass on to 11 a.m., then to 1 p.m. At other times I would pray quietly in other tongues. The clock progressed past 3 p.m. Often I would read select verses from my Bible and meditate on them. Eventually the clock drew near to the 5:00 hour. I had now been waiting on the Lord for almost eight hours, and although I had been greatly refreshed from all the spiritually edifying activities, the Lord had still not spoken a single word to me.

As I looked out the window, I saw my wife's white car ascending up the mountain toward our home. She soon arrived at the top of our long driveway and was getting ready to make the sharp turn to come down the driveway toward the house. Because I've driven it so many times, I know that it takes exactly two minutes to reach the house once you make that turn. With only two minutes left of alone time with the Lord before the family arrived, it was then that God decided to talk to me! Suddenly, revelation knowledge began to flood into my spirit like a mighty river. He shared things with me so fast but yet in a way that it all sank in firmly. It felt like standing beneath a fast-flowing waterfall with my mouth open. With only 15 seconds to spare I asked the Lord, "Why did You wait for so long before speaking to me? I've been here all day."

He replied, "Because I enjoyed your company today, and I wanted you to stay with Me as long as possible."

I was floored by His comment. It was then that the front door flew open and I heard, "Hi Daddy, I'm home!" as my daughter joyfully entered the house. Now, with a full heart and the renewed strength of an eagle, it was time to turn my attention to the needs of others.

We need to also be aware of the blessing that comes from waiting *for* the Lord. This is expressed clearly to us by the prophet Isaiah in the following verses.

> ***Therefore the Lord will wait, that He may be gracious to you;*** *and therefore He will be exalted, that He may have mercy on you. For the Lord is a God of justice;* ***blessed are all those who wait for Him*** (Isaiah 30:18).

The purpose of God answering prayer and coordinating the manifestation of His promises toward us in a way that may seem to take longer than what we would like, is that He wants to be good to us in the best possible way. To endeavor to rush God is to find fault with God. When we are frustrated by God's timing, it reveals our own impatience and lack of trust. God's primary purpose of waiting is to be good to us. After all, would you rather have a delicious, home-cooked, slowly-made meal or a cheap and greasy fast-food meal that is only eaten because of a rushed situation? When we wait with the right frame of heart, I have discovered that God will then often give to us something better than what we asked for or were even aware existed.

> Waiting is almost a lost art. Everything is done in a hurry. So many things require only the pushing of a button, but there is no button to push—no magic formula—no "royal road"—to power with God. The man who has waited upon God commands the demon to depart, and the tormented one is free. The man who hasn't time to "waste" in waiting speaks the same words, seems to do the same things, but nothing happens. Waiting upon God is not wasted time, although it many times may seem to you as well as to others that you are doing nothing. Waiting on God includes fasting, prayer, and just plain waiting. When we pray, we talk to God, but when you have prayed until there seems to be nothing more to say, then you need to wait for an answer. Let God speak to you. —A.A. Allen

Recently I went to India to film television programs for a large Christian television network. It was a ten-day trip that involved filming a full year's worth of programs in only five days. It's basically a routine of shooting two programs that last 30 minutes each, taking a tea break, and then shooting two more programs, followed by another tea break, and repeating this all day long with a short lunch break, five days in a row. It's fun because there are so many shows to do I never use notes. I just stand up, open my Bible, and preach whatever message comes to me extemporaneously by the Spirit. Sometimes I'll tell my translator what the Scripture verse will be only one minute before the cameras roll. It's important to be full of the Word of God in our hearts so that when we have opportunity to share it, we don't have to say, "I'm sorry, I can't help you; let me call my pastor and see if he can explain it to you." We should always be prepared, whether in season or out of season, to minister the Word.

Each day after the recordings were completed, I would return to the nice hotel where I was staying. While on this trip, it seemed as if an overwhelming desire to build my own new television studio was weighing heavy on my heart. In our former offices, we had a beautiful television studio that took a lot of time, effort, and money to assemble, but it was all taken down when we were blessed to buy our own church building and move into it. Because of the recent move and ongoing efforts of remodeling of the church building, we were forced in the interim to use a very low-quality television set and I was not pleased with its quality. While in India I thought, "When I get back home I'm going to build a small television studio close to the church in that open area of the grass field." I began to pray fervently toward this goal with a heart to want to see more people around the world reached with the Gospel. Each morning, I would arise hours before sunup, and after filming in the India studio I would return to the hotel and continue to pray fervently for several more hours toward this desire before going to bed.

Toward the end of the week as filming was nearing completion, I was in the studio recording a live message. The cameras were rolling, the sound engineers were monitoring audio and technical feedback from the sound-room which looked into the studio, and the camera engineers were operating the cameras. While preaching my interpreter stood next to me as he fluently translated my English message into the Tamil language. Every time I would say a few sentences I would pause to give him time to interpret. Right in the middle of my preaching, a man walked into the recording studio wearing a white gown that reached all the way to his feet. I could clearly see that he had leather sandals on his feet, but I could not see his face because the studio lights were shining directly in my eyes. He went and sat down on a couch and listened to me preach.

The first thought that came to me when this man walked in was, "I can't believe someone slipped in during a live recording. Usually the camera team would never allow that." The television studio was very modern with special security features. To get into the studio you had to have an appointment, sign in with the secretary, pass by a security guard, go down a hallway and pass through two successive doors that could only be unlocked with a laser scanner that verified your identity through a laser beam that scanned your fingerprint. As the man in the white gown sat on the other side of the recording studio, I realized the reason I couldn't see His face was not because of the glare of the studio lights, but rather because of the light emitting from His face. It was then I realized that it was the Lord Jesus who had come by to hear me preach!

The Lord sat in the studio and listened to my full message. As soon as the message ended and the cameraman yelled, "Cut," I stepped forward and out from the lights and looked toward the couch, but there was no one there. While preaching I saw Him so clearly that I thought surely the film crew must have seen Him as well, but I realized I was the only one. There were a few more recordings scheduled for me to do before lunch, but never before was I in such a hurry to finish and take my lunch break so that I could pray and discern the purpose for the Lord's visit. Fortunately, when lunchtime arrived the film director asked me if I would be OK with taking an extended lunch break due to some extra work that the team needed to do on some equipment. "Sure," I replied, knowing that this would allow me a little longer to pray.

An assistant ushered me to a separate room where I could eat my turkey and cheese sandwich that he had picked up for me at Subway, although it didn't have the American taste to it with the curry flavor infused into it. After finishing my meal, I spent time studying the Word for the upcoming messages, as well as inquiring of the Lord for His reason for visiting me. Although He did not give me a specific answer during my lunch break, I knew it was forthcoming.

Once I was back into the studio, I was refreshed and ready to go. With the cameras rolling, I jumped into two more successive messages to build faith in the hearts of God's people. Knowing my routine well, I then went to sit down for a hot tea. As soon as I sat on the couch (in the same spot where the Lord sat earlier) I put my Bible down and it fell open to a certain page. As it did, a verse appeared to become highlighted and lifted up off the page and stood suspended in the air. My startled eyes fell upon the Scripture, as I read:

Wait on the Lord and keep His way, and He shall exalt you to inherit the land... (Psalms 37:34).

When I saw this Scripture I knew for a certainty the reason for the Lord's visit. Three years earlier, I received a promise from the Lord about eventually acquiring a special piece of property for the ministry. It was this exact verse that the Lord gave me three years earlier to use with my faith in order to hold onto the promise of God. For the past three years, I had waited patiently for this promise to be fulfilled with the intention of building our new television recording studio and ministry offices upon this land. Although I do not yet know the specific location of this land, I know that at the right time it will be revealed to me. Through the Lord's visit to me in India, He spoke to me to, "Wait, and do not build your television studio on the present church property, but rather on the land of promise which you will soon acquire. For the ministry offices and studio which you will build will be much larger than you have formerly envisioned, so wait for Me so that it may be built according to the plan that I will give to you."

It's important that we wait and not get ahead of God in our timing. If we rush God and do our own thing, we attempt to do it in our own strength and will have limited results, or worse yet, failed results.

Unless the Lord builds the house, they labor in vain who build it... (Psalms 127:1).

So for now, we continue to wait, pray, and exercise our faith for the fullness of this prophetic word to come to pass.

For since the beginning of the world men have not heard nor perceived by the ear, nor has the eye seen any God besides You, who acts for the one who waits for Him (Isaiah 64:4).

When you wait for God, then you are promised that He will act for you. The word *act* means that God will "work and go into action" for you. When you fast and pray it seems like everything slows down. One thing, however, that speeds up is God going to work on your behalf. Even while you sleep at night, God will be working and acting for you. Your decision to not try and rush God, but to rather trust Him for His best to be done in your life, allows the Lord to give you His very best. Waiting for Him through prayer and fasting will allow your spiritual ears to hear things you have not heard before. Your spiritual eyes will open in a new way, causing you to see into a greater dimension of God. This is what happens when you humble yourself and wait for Him. Those wonderful things which God has prepared for you will become apparent, much to your great delight.

> *But as it is written: "Eye has not seen, nor ear heard, nor have entered into the heart of man the things which God has prepared for those who love Him"* (1 Corinthians 2:9).

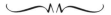

If God has called you into a full time ministry of healing the sick and casting out devils, He usually gives you time to give yourselves to fasting and prayer. —W.V. Grant, Sr.

Paul directly quoted from Isaiah as he wrote the above verse, but he changed it a little bit in light of the New Covenant of love and grace we now are in. These Scriptures both emphasize seeing and hearing (and experiencing) the amazing things which God has prepared for us. Isaiah said these wonderful things are revealed for *those who wait for God.* Paul said it is prepared for *those who love God.* The revelation that the Holy Spirit is trying to convey to us through these two men is that *if you love God, you will wait for Him.* If you love God you will fast and pray, thus causing you to slow down and hear and see from God the things which He has prepared for you. Your spiritual eyes and ears will pick up on things that cannot be grasped when in a rush. You will make the right decisions. You will choose the right path. You will marry the right person. You will make the right investment. You will see results in your prayer life. You will receive the revelations from God that the Holy Spirit desires to impart, yes, even the deep things of God. It comes to those who wait for Him and thus demonstrate that they love Him.

As you *wait on the Lord* and also *wait for the Lord,* you will then discover the pleasure of *waiting with the Lord. Waiting with the Lord* denotes those sacred times when the Lord responds to our seeking Him. There comes an unmistakable awareness that God has drawn near and is in our midst. Often this will involve visions, angelic visitations, or appearances of the Lord Jesus. Walter Beuttler was a prophet and teacher who traveled to over 100 countries teaching on the manifest Presence of God. For many years, Brother Beuttler would wait on the Lord in the middle of the night, often between the hours of 2:00 a.m. to 5:00 a.m. He once shared an experience of how the Lord came to him in response to his earnest pursuit of seeking God in the late night hours.

> One night I clearly perceived in my spirit, there was no sound or voice. I clearly perceived in my spirit the Lord coming up from behind me. I was sitting in a chair. He was coming up from behind, walking toward me. Now the Lord hears what I'm saying. He knows it's the truth. I wouldn't dare tell you a fib. The Lord bent over me from behind like this (demonstrated). I was facing this way, and He came up like this, and He bent over me. I could perceive He bent His head and looked down, and folks, as sure as you sit here, as sure as God hears my every word, I had the feeling as though it were literally so, of drops falling on my head. I could feel like drops fall on my head—several. I do not know how many, not many but several. I had the clearest (How strong can I make this?), most positive knowledge instinctively conveyed by the Spirit, that what I felt were the tears of the

Lord's appreciation falling on my head. I'm not saying they were literal tears. They were a manifestation of His presence. He let me feel them. I'm not saying they were literal, but they were as real as though they were.

They were the tears of the Lord's appreciation that someone would be up night after night, for a time only, to sit there in a holy solemnity. He wanted me to know the depth of the appreciation of His heart for getting up during the night to keep a holy solemnity. These are some of the treasures of the riches of the knowledge of God that God has for those whose heart and spirit is poised God ward—a holy solemnity.[1]

Waiting with the Lord allows us to experience those special times when the Lord comes with His tangible presence. During these times you may not "see" the Lord, but you are able to clearly discern His Presence. After all, if He is there is it even necessary for us to see Him? No, often the Lord comes with His Presence, which is just the same as if you saw Him sitting there.

Recently I flew home on a cross-country plane flight. There were two ladies sitting in front of me who were both blind. Their "seeing-eye dogs" were lying quietly on the floor of the plane as we settled in for a long flight. Despite the two women being completely blind, they still carried on an extended conversation and enjoyed one another's company. The point I want to make is that even though they were blind, they still had fellowship and communication. When the Lord comes to visit you, it is possible that you may not see Him, but rather that you *perceive* Him. He will speak to you just as a close friend would. From these times of waiting *on* the Lord and then progressing to waiting *for* the Lord thus culminating into distinctive sessions of waiting *with* the Lord, you will experience the nuclear power of God and walk in the realm of the miraculous.

A short time ago, I returned from a trip in which I ministered in a meeting in California. While there, a woman brought a particular man to my meeting. Now old in age, this man was known throughout the entire community as the vilest sinner. He had formerly been in prison. He was a professional hit man who murdered people for money. He was a drug user, sexual pervert, and former owner of seven pornography stores. His list of sins was truly piled up to Heaven. Other ministers had held meetings here before, but this man refused to attend any previous meetings yet he decided to come to mine. The first night he heard me preach he told the person who brought him, "That preacher is an absolute nut; he's crazy!"

But on the second night of the meeting, the power of God was mightily demonstrated as people were miraculously healed. When this man saw the power of God, his heart for the first time in his life was softened. Because he himself was suffering with several major illnesses, I asked him if he would allow me to pray for him. He responded with a firm, "Yes."

When I prayed for him, he was touched by God's healing power. Immediately, I took advantage of the open door, knowing that divine healing is the dinner bell for the lost. I publicly asked him if he wanted to receive Jesus as his Lord and Savior, and he responded that he did. I led him in the sinner's prayer, and Jesus saved him right then and there. When I took my hand off of him after the prayer, people were amazed as the man's entire countenance changed! Gone was the depraved look on his face—now there was a new look of complete peace and kindness. He looked like he was lit up from the inside with a light bulb.

We were all deeply humbled by God's mighty power to save even the most loathsome person. On the final night of my meetings, this man was filled with the joy of the Lord as he would raise his hands and worship God. Again, a renewed appreciation for the power of Christ's saving blood came over the people in the meeting as we witnessed the dramatic change in this man's life. The meeting ended with a glorious release of God's Spirit upon all of us, including our newly-saved brother in the Lord.

Why do these things happen in my meetings? They happen because I take time to fast, pray, and wait on the Lord. Before the meetings ever started, they told me about this man and I began to spend entire days in prayer for the meetings, dialing down my food intake to only eating almonds and cashews while drinking just water and an occasional coffee. These same types of miracle *will happen for anyone* who will follow the biblical pattern. If we want Pentecostal results like we see in the Book of Acts, then we must apply Pentecostal methods. The rewards justify the sacrifices of sincere and diligent prayers that we offer up to God. So make time to seek the Lord while He may be found. Pursue Him with all of your heart. He will come and visit you. He will wait *with* you and empower you to succeed in everything you put your hand to.

Endnote

1. Walter Beuttler, "A Holy Solemnity" (From a taped transcript spoken in the late 1960s, early 1970s. Transcribed by Mrs. Pearl Ray of Harvest Age Ministries.

CHAPTER NINE

REMEMBER THE POOR

ISAIAH 58 IS, IN MY OPINION, the greatest teaching in the Word of God on the proper guidelines concerning fasting. The entire chapter deals with the motives and sincerity for fasting. God confirms in this chapter that He will do wonderful breakthroughs for the person who fasts with the right heart. The promises are actually staggering, as almost every possible need is addressed with a sure remedy guaranteed when prayer and fasting are done in the right frame of heart. Please read through this following chapter slowly and consider the promises that God extends to you through prayer and fasting.

> *Cry aloud, spare not; lift up your voice like a trumpet; tell My people their transgression, and the house of Jacob their sins. Yet they seek Me daily, and delight to know My ways, as a nation that did righteousness, and did not forsake the ordinance of their God. They ask of Me the ordinances of justice; they take delight in approaching God. "Why have we fasted," they say,*

"and You have not seen? Why have we afflicted our souls, and You take no notice?"

In fact, in the day of your fast you find pleasure, and exploit all your laborers. Indeed you fast for strife and debate, and to strike with the fist of wickedness. You will not fast as you do this day, to make your voice heard on high. Is it a fast that I have chosen, a day for a man to afflict his soul? Is it to bow down his head like a bulrush, and to spread out sackcloth and ashes? Would you call this a fast, and an acceptable day to the Lord?

Is this not the fast that I have chosen: to loose the bonds of wickedness, to undo the heavy burdens, to let the oppressed go free, and that you break every yoke? Is it not to share your bread with the hungry, and that you bring to your house the poor who are cast out; when you see the naked, that you cover him, and not hide yourself from your own flesh? Then your light shall break forth like the morning, your healing shall spring forth speedily, and your righteousness shall go before you; the glory of the Lord shall be your rear guard. Then you shall call, and the Lord will answer; you shall cry, and He will say, "Here I am."

If you take away the yoke from your midst, the pointing of the finger, and speaking wickedness, if you extend your soul to the hungry and satisfy the afflicted soul, then your light shall dawn in the darkness, and your darkness shall be as the noonday. The Lord will guide you continually, and satisfy your soul in drought, and strengthen your bones; you shall be like a watered garden, and like a spring of water, whose waters do not fail. Those from among you shall build the old waste places; you shall raise up the foundations of many generations; and you shall be called the Repairer of the Breach, the Restorer of Streets to Dwell In.

If you turn away your foot from the Sabbath, from doing your pleasure on My holy day, and call the Sabbath a delight, the holy day of the Lord honorable, and shall honor Him, not doing your own ways, nor finding your own pleasure, nor speaking your own words, then you shall delight yourself in the Lord; and I will cause you to ride on the high hills of the earth, and feed you with the heritage of Jacob your father. The mouth of the Lord has spoken.

Whenever you do a fast I recommend that you spend time often meditating on Isaiah 58. This chapter will prove to be a great source of hope and strength for you while fasting. There is a special emphasis given regarding helping the poor, hungry, naked, and needy. Many people have forgotten the poor. When you fast, a divine compassion from God will enter your heart and you will begin to view the poor with new concern.

Job was a man in the Bible who had great pity and care for the poor. Unfortunately, the book of Job has been so mis-taught and viewed in such a negative light that most Christians don't even want to read the book, considering it gloomy and irrelevant. But it is one of the most wonderful books in the Bible. The fact that many believers stay away from this book should be a big hint to you that there must be some special gems in it hidden by the Lord for those who are spiritually-minded. When the devil spoke to the Lord about Job and basically said the only reason Job served Him was because of the blessings received through obedience, then God gave the devil freedom to test Job. God was proud of Job; he was the best God had, and God trusted Job. It is true that all the blessings Job walked in were a direct result of God's blessing upon his life, but Job clung to the Lord even when he lost everything.

Job was a very, very wealthy man. Today some believers often talk about Joseph, who ended up in a place of powerful influence. For some reason, to believers the life of Joseph seems attractive and inspirational—which it most certainly is. So Joseph receives much attention within Christian investing circles while Job is rarely mentioned. But Joseph and Job walked in two different types of anointing. Joseph represents corporate wealth. Job represents personal wealth.

Bill Gates helped to make many people millionaires through the corporation he built known as Microsoft. I have a friend who made millions of dollars years back because he worked for Microsoft when it was still a small company. He was given stock options in the company, and when the company became successful, he one day cashed in his shares for several million dollars. This happened to a number of people. Bill Gates used his wisdom to develop a technology that caused many others to become wealthy within his corporation.

One thing more I would mention concerning fasting and prayer, wherein I think there has been a neglect in ministers; and that is, that although they recommend and much insist on the duty of secret prayer, in their preaching; so little is said about secret fasting. It is a duty recommended by our Savior to His followers, just in the like manner as secret prayer is; as may be seen by comparing the 5th and 6th verses of the 6th chapter of Matthew with verses 16-18. Though I don't suppose that secret fasting is to be practiced in a stated manner and steady course as secret prayer, yet it seems to me 'tis a duty that all professing Christians should practice, and frequently practice. —Jonathan Edwards

Within Christian investment circles, I sometimes hear investment groups call themselves with names like the *Joseph Group*, *Joseph Club*, or some other name identifying them with the successful creation of wealth that Joseph was responsible for overseeing. However, I don't think I have ever seen any Christian investors call their group the *Job Club* or the *Job Investment Organization*. We need to understand the anointing of God's Spirit for corporate wealth as well as the anointing that rested upon Job for personal wealth. God has a different anointing for different types of people, and He has a *specific* path that He will lead you on.

Job could be compared to Warren Buffet of our modern day and time. Warren Buffet is known for having amassed great personal wealth through wise business decisions that are based on solid ethical principles. Because he lives in Omaha, Nebraska, he is known as the "Oracle of Omaha." Well, in a similar way Job was the financial "Oracle of Uz." When Job spoke, he was like that old E.F. Hutton commercial where everybody else in the room would immediately become silent to carefully listen to Mr. Hutton's words of financial wisdom.

When I went out to the gate by the city, when I took my seat in the open square, the young men saw me and hid, and the aged arose and stood; the princes refrained from talking, and put their hand on their mouth; the voice of nobles was hushed, and their tongue stuck to the roof of their mouth (Job 29:7-10).

Job was the "Financial Guru of the East." He commanded attention and respect at the gate of his city where the elders met and held a reputation of greatness that was extended throughout the entire Middle East. He used his personal wealth as godly leverage to influence others to also serve God and to live holy lives. Despite his enormous wealth, he still had a great heart of compassion for the poor and needy. When Job went through his great trial, his three friends were suspicious about his character and suggested to him that the reason for his trial was because he was committing ungodly acts. With great effort and conviction, Job refuted their statements and gave a strong defense in his case.

Oh, that I were as in months past, as in the days when God watched over me (Job 29:2).

When my steps were bathed with cream, and the rock poured out rivers of oil for me! (Job 29:6)

In these verses Job acknowledged the source of his blessing. Job knew that it was God who was multiplying his finances and bringing increase to his many different business ventures. Job says that his *steps were bathed in cream.* That is a statement which denotes how God caused everything to produce bountifully in his life. Everything about Job's huge financial empire was well-oiled and operated smoothly, as Job reveals by saying the *rock poured out rivers of oil for me.* Job understood covenant wealth and knew he had a responsibility to use this wealth to also minister to the needs of others.

I delivered the poor who cried out, the fatherless and the one who had no helper. The blessing of a perishing man came upon me, and I caused the widow's heart to sing for joy. I put on righteousness, and it clothed me; my justice was like a robe and a turban. I was eyes to the blind, and I was feet to the lame. I was a father to the poor, and I searched out the case that I did not know. I broke the fangs of the wicked, and plucked the victim from his teeth (Job 29:12-17).

Here we see that Job helped countless people in need. He was aggressive in taking action, even seeking out those he could help. He didn't sit back and just wait for someone to ask for help, he went looking to see who he could help. Back in those days, if you could not pay your debt then the debt collectors would not only take possession of your home and property, they also had the legal right to take you and all your children into their ownership and force you into slavery. Job would search out these types of cases. He would get into his Rolls Royce (i.e. his camel—the richest man in the East did not drive a scooter) and drive his car over to the slave auction. The wolves (debt collectors) were licking their lips with drool coming off of their fangs as they gloated over another family about to be split apart and auctioned off into slavery. Right at the last moment Job would step in there, pay off the indebtedness owed, and deliver entire families, once again breaking the *teeth of the wicked*. He would *pluck the victim right out of the mouth* of the debt collector, just like a shepherd would grab a sheep out of the mouth of a predator lion. Did you know this about Job? There's more you should probably be aware of regarding Job.

> *Have I not wept for him who was in trouble? Has not my soul grieved for the poor?* (Job 30:25)

Job had compassion and a sincere care for the poor. His righteous deeds were not fabricated acts done to get on the latest magazine cover. His motives were pure; he was doing this because he loved the Lord.

> *If I have kept the poor from their desire, or caused the eyes of the widow to fail, or eaten my morsel by myself, so that the fatherless could not eat of it (But from my youth I reared him as a father, and from my mother's womb I guided the widow); if I have seen anyone perish for lack of clothing, or any poor man without covering; if his heart has not blessed me, and if he was not warmed with the fleece of my sheep; if I have raised my hand against the fatherless, when I saw I had help in the gate; then let my arm fall from my shoulder, let my arm be torn from the socket* (Job 31:16-22).

Job owned 7,000 sheep. From this great flock he would take the wool from some and have coats made, and then give coats to the poor who had none. There are a lot of nice things to wear in this world, but on a cold day it's hard to beat a warm wool garment. There certainly were those critics who must have said, "He has too many sheep. All he cares about is money." But those people had no clue of the kind of man that Job really was. While the critics were busy posting mean articles on the Internet complaining about his great prosperity, he was out busily ministering the love of God to the poor in a tangible way.

Job reminds me of Charles Spurgeon who also had his share of critics. Charles Spurgeon had a large orphanage. He also pastored a church that had 10,000 members. Once a year, Spurgeon used to preach for "his orphans." At that great meeting, many would come to hear the famous preacher, and an offering would be received for his orphanage. After one of these meetings, he is reputed to have been leaving the building where the service had taken place when a man accosted him with the charge, "Why, Mr. Spurgeon, I thought you preached for souls and not for money!"

As the story goes, Spurgeon gravely replied, "Why, Sir, normally I do preach for souls and not for money. But my orphans can't eat souls, and if they did, my brother, it would take at least four the size of yours to give one of them a square meal!" My prayer is, "Lord, make me like Job and Charles Spurgeon!"

If I fail to spend two hours in prayer each morning, the devil gets the victory through the day. I have so much business I cannot get on without spending three hours daily in prayer. —Martin Luther

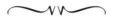

Earlier today my wife and I had the immense delight of boxing up 500 pairs of new shoes. We were going to wait for the rest of our ministry helps team to arrive and assist us, but we started early and it gave us so much joy in doing this work that we finished before our helpers arrived. Tomorrow we will drive these large boxes to a loading dock so that the truck can transport them to a ship which will then carry these shoes to the Republic of Congo in Africa. Within a few weeks there will be 500 children running around in brand new shoes who are now barefoot. Years ago, I made up my mind that I refuse to be poor. The blessing of the Lord makes me rich, and God adds no sorrow with it. It's impossible to help others when you are defeated. The poor cannot deliver the poor. God desires for *you* to be a financial champion and to walk in His kingly anointing.

> *For if because of one man's trespass (lapse, offense) death reigned through that one, much more surely will those who receive [God's] overflowing grace (unmerited favor) and the free gift of righteousness [putting them into right standing with Himself]* **reign as kings in life** *through the one Man Jesus Christ (the Messiah, the Anointed One)* (Romans 5:17 AMP).

Job made it through his trial and had his former possessions restored to him—double. He ended up with 14,000 sheep, 6,000 camels, 1,000 yoke of oxen, and 1,000 female donkeys. That's a total of 22,000 animals. This would also indicate that Job employed a large work force to take care of these animals and to sell certain ones, and he certainly would have owned a large amount of land. Through honoring God and seeking Him through prayer and fasting, our vision can be enlarged to minister effectively with a heart of compassion. Job was a trendsetter who many have successfully emulated.

In order to help the poor and reach the multitude of souls in the world with the Gospel of Jesus Christ, we must overcome a scarcity mentality. Overcoming a scarcity mentality basically comes down to making a choice between living in the blessing or living in the curse.

> *And if it seems evil to you to serve the Lord, choose for yourselves this day whom you will serve, whether the gods which your fathers served that were on the other side of the River, or the gods of the Amorites, in whose land you dwell. But as for me and my house, we will serve the Lord* (Joshua 24:15).

When Joshua boldly confessed that he and his house would serve the Lord, he was referring to more than his immediate house consisting of his wife and children. He was referring to his clan, or tribe. Twelve tribes made up the nation of Israel. There are many different "tribes" in the Body of Christ, with various denominational and non-denominational churches. Joshua spoke on behalf of his tribe, Ephraim, and emphatically expressed the necessity of obeying God and thus walking in His blessings. He strongly urged the Israelites to serve the Lord so that they would be protected from the curse in the earth. Obedience brings the blessings of God. Sin and disobedience to God's Word gives the devil a legal right to enter in with destructive power.

When Joshua and Caleb brought back a good report from having spied out the Promised Land, the other ten tribal leaders persuaded the people with their negative view of the situation, which God described as being an evil report (see Num. 14:37). Not everyone in the twelve tribes was in mutual agreement. Not everyone in the Church today is in agreement either concerning certain teachings. In our church, I emphasize the need for our members to believe God for abundance so that we can give to the poor and support the work of spreading the Gospel throughout the earth by means of the printed page, Internet, and television. I specifically pray for my church members and ministry partners that God prosper them in every area of their lives, including their finances.

Beloved, I pray that you may prosper [have good success] in all things and be in health, just as your soul prospers (3 John 2).

Some ministers agree with a scarcity mentality. It's a choice that they choose to make. But I believe that whatever views a person holds to, they should practice what they preach. If one believes in living a life of scarcity and poverty, then we should see that evidenced in their life. If a preacher says, "It is God's will for you to be poor," then you should verify if *he* practices that. In other words, if a preacher says you are supposed to be poor, then you need to inquire and see what type of car that preacher drives. Actually, if he says it is God's will to be poor, he should not even own a car. He should glory in scarcity and lack and should walk or ride a bicycle everywhere he goes. If he really practices what he preaches, he would consider owning a car to be an expression of "vanity" and "worldliness." But I have never seen any preacher give up their car or give away their house in order to live on the street so that they might hold to the teaching that "to be poor is to be holy." In fact, most that criticize and preach against the "prosperity gospel" live in nice, comfortable homes and drive good vehicles. The critics don't even practice what they preach. This is because everyone has an inherent sense to know that scarcity and poverty are not good.

There is something intrinsically evil about sickness, disease, scarcity, poverty, famine, lack, and starvation that cause people to want to avoid it. This is encoded within our spiritual DNA the same way we are encoded by God to know to not go out and pick up a cobra snake or play with a wolverine.

Once while shopping in a store I engaged a Christian man in conversation as he shared with me that he didn't have any extra money beyond just the basic ability to pay his bills. With a pious and religious look he then quoted me what he thought to be a verse from the Holy Bible: "God will meet your needs, but that is all He will do."

In response I said, "That's an interesting verse; where is that in the Bible?"

He replied, "I don't know where it's at, but that's what the preacher told us in church, although I haven't been able to find the verse yet."

Seeing an opportunity to shed some light I said, "Well, don't bother wasting your time looking for it because it's *not* in there. However, there is a verse that I do know that *is* in there." At that point I took out my small New Testament, which also included the book of Psalms and Proverbs, that I was carrying in my back pocket. Opening my Bible, I asked him to read the following verse out loud.

*Delight yourself also in the Lord, and He shall **give you the desires of your heart*** (Psalm 37:4).

Upon reading what God had to say about the situation I asked him, "What do you think about that?"

He responded with a blushed look of surprise, appearing a little bit embarrassed as he slowly said, "Whoa, I never knew that was in there." Before leaving I encouraged him that there were lots of other verses just like that one spread liberally throughout the Bible. God desires for you to walk in a position of overflow,

160

not scarcity and lack. God not only wants to meet your *needs,* He wants to give you the *desires* of your heart.

You overcome a scarcity mentality by believing what the Word of God says about His will for your life and future. You overcome a scarcity mentality by not daily viewing four hours of bad news on television which focuses on recession, job lay-offs, and unemployment statistics. But instead you choose to read and confess what the Word of God says rightfully belongs to you as a child of God. Jesus was correct when He said that we would always have the poor among us. But that doesn't mean *you* have to be poor.

There was in the Lord's time and there are in our modern day countless believers who do not know the covenant (contract) they have with their God. Even though they are entitled to the blessings of God, they never experience them because they do not know their legal rights that the Word says they have. Their lack of knowledge robs them of their ability to receive the blessings of God through faith.

The Old Testament saints had a covenant of circumcision that God established through Abraham. As New Covenant saints (saints with a new written contract) we have a better covenant (contract) established by the blood of the Lord Jesus. Abraham knew God by divine revelation as Jehovah Jireh (The Lord Your Provider). Through the New Covenant you now have eternal life and victory over sin and the curse, along with the blessings of Abraham also.

*Christ has redeemed us from the curse of the law, having become a curse for us (for it is written, "Cursed is everyone who hangs on a tree"), that the **blessing of Abraham might come upon the Gentiles in Christ Jesus,** that we might receive the promise of the Spirit through faith* (Galatians 3:13-14).

161

To overcome a scarcity mentality you to need to meditate upon the truth that *you have a Jehovah Jireh in your life!* Refuse lack and scarcity. Refuse sin and disobedience which would release the curse into your life. Live a life that honors God where you walk in the fear of the Lord and diligently study and meditate on the Word so that you walk in all the commandments of God. Confess, believe, and acknowledge that God is a good and kind God and that he is your Jehovah Jireh. Allow Jehovah Jireh to lift you higher and move you into the position of being a Kingdom giver.

> *I have shown you in every way, by laboring like this, that you must support the weak. And remember the words of the Lord Jesus, that He said, "It is more blessed to give than to receive"* (Acts 20:35).

As you meditate upon God's Word and do your daily work with all of your might as doing it unto the Lord, your thinking will change and you will become a more effective and productive believer within the Kingdom of God. Thoughts of scarcity will be replaced with thoughts of plenty, and you will influence many lives to accept Christ in your witness for Jesus. God's blessing will work in your life, causing you to be fruitful and productive in all that you put your hands to. Let your thoughts always agree with the Word of God, as reflected in the following verse.

> *The **thoughts** of the diligent tend only to **plenteousness**...* (Proverbs 21:5 KJV).

In the New Testament we see examples of those who gave out of their abundance to minister to others. They had soft hearts and set godly patterns for us to follow. When you fast and pray, you will find the Holy Spirit engrafting into you a heart like the Good Samaritan. In Luke 10, we find the following exchange between Jesus and an expert in the Mosaic law.

And behold, a certain lawyer stood up and tested Him, saying, "Teacher, what shall I do to inherit eternal life?" He said to him, "What is written in the law? What is your reading of it?" (Luke 10:25-26)

Often these lawyers were called upon to settle legal issues. The lawyer stood up to test Jesus with a question. By standing up he displayed a common greeting of respect toward Jesus. He then said, *"Teacher, what shall I do to inherit eternal life?"* Jesus responds by asking, *"What is written in the law? What is your reading of it?"* If many believers today did what Jesus suggested they would solve many of their problems very quickly. If we would open our Bibles and study them thoroughly, we would know exactly what to do. The answers are already in the Book, we just need to read for ourselves and see what God says about the situation. For whatever question we may have, there is an answer somewhere for it in the Bible.

So he answered and said, "'You shall love the Lord your God with all your heart, with all your soul, with all your strength, and with all your mind,' and 'your neighbor as yourself.'" And He said to him, "You have answered rightly; do this and you will live." But he, wanting to justify himself, said to Jesus, "And who is my neighbor?" (Luke 10:27-29).

The lawyer is convinced of his own self-righteousness, so he endeavors to justify himself. He does not humble himself and say, "How do I love my neighbor? Please teach me." Instead, he uses his lawyer mentality and presents a technical question to Jesus while continuing to exude confidence that his own righteousness is an airtight case. Jesus does not respond in a traditional way by suggesting that your neighbor is simply the person who lives next door or down the street, or someone who has the same skin color.

Then Jesus answered and said: "A certain man went down from Jerusalem to Jericho, and fell among thieves, who stripped him of his clothing, wounded him, and departed, leaving him half dead" (Luke 10:30).

The city of Jerusalem sits on a hill. There is a road that goes down from Jerusalem to Jericho. The road is 17 miles long and has a drop in elevation of 3,000 feet. For many years, this route was known as being very hazardous because of thieves and robbers. Jesus does not tell us much about the man who took this journey, but we can assume that because Jesus was speaking to a Jewish audience, then the man who took the journey would be a Jewish man. Having fallen among thieves, he was stripped of his clothes, wounded, and left half dead. If he didn't get help soon, he would not be half dead but fully dead. The thieves most likely tried to kill him and perhaps thought they had, with the intent of not having a witness who could later identify them for the crime. Lying naked in the beating sun with life quickly slipping away, his only hope for survival lay in the hands of some compassionate person.

Now by chance a certain priest came down that road. And when he saw him, he passed by on the other side (Luke 10:31).

We can suspect the priest was riding, because he was in the upper classes of society. The poor couldn't afford a horse or donkey, so they walked. The priest went to the other side because he didn't want to risk becoming ceremonially unclean. The beaten man was lying naked. Throughout history you can usually tell a person's social status and even nationality by the type of clothing worn. The priest couldn't tell from a distance if the man was a Jew or Gentile, rich or poor, or even dead or alive. He was not allowed to go within four cubits of a dead person. To verify if he was alive, he would have needed to touch and examine him. If the man were dead, then the priest would have to go through an

elaborate cleansing process that was time-consuming and finan-
cially costly. While the priest would be in the cleansing process,
he could not receive nor eat tithes. He also would have to purchase a red heifer and complete the burning procedure which
took a full week. On top of it all, the priests were supposed to be
the example to the people of one who kept the law. Becoming
defiled would mean he would have to publicly stand at the Eastern Gate with other unclean people. This could potentially look
embarrassing to his peers and perhaps jeopardize his climbing
up the job ladder, and he would be snickered at by some of the
other unclean people as they would think, "Hmmm, I wonder
what he did?" The priest decided to play it safe, and he went
around the wounded man and continued on his journey. If you
were this priest in this situation, what would you have done?

Someone asked Finney what kind of man this
Father Nash was. "We never see him," they said.
"He doesn't enter into any of the meetings."

Finney replied, "Like anybody who does a lot of
praying, Father Nash is a very quiet person." Show
me a person who is always talking and I'll show
you a Christian who never does much praying. —
Charles Finney

Rendering aid to others never seems to come at a convenient
time. The priest simply could have been in a hurry to catch the
latest movie at the new theater down in Jericho. By stopping to

help he could have risked missing the movie previews before the show started. I know that sounds silly, but it will almost always pose an inconvenience when God gives you an opportunity to extend your soul to help someone in need. I wish it were always easy, but it never seems to work out like that. Often it requires some type of sacrifice and compassion.

After ministering in a church in Uganda several years back, I asked the pastor how he was able to acquire the beautiful land upon which his church, orphanage, and Bible school were built. It was apparent the pastor did not have much money, so how could he ever get such a large and beautiful piece of property? He shared his story with me by saying, "Pastor Steven, there was an elderly woman in my church who became very ill. She needed medical help, but the nearest hospital was eleven miles away. Seeing the old woman in agonizing pain and not having any means of transportation, I did the only thing that was possible for me to do. I took a wheelbarrow and placed her in it, and pushed her down a dirt road in the wheelbarrow all the way to the hospital. Once we arrived there, she received the necessary help and soon recovered from her illness. Two years later she died peacefully, and to my great shock I discovered that in her will she had deeded all her property to me! Today all of our ministry facilities are on this property, and we still have much room for more future growth." This dear pastor had a heart of compassion, unlike the priest in our story.

As the sun continued to beat down on the wounded Jewish man, a few scraggly buzzards began to gather on some nearby boulders as they anticipated that it wouldn't be too much longer until mealtime.

Likewise a Levite, when he arrived at the place, came and looked, and passed by on the other side (Luke 10:32).

166

The beaten man has another opportunity for rescue, but it appears his SOS distress beacon was not working properly. This time a Levite passed by. The priests were descendants of Aaron. The Levites were descendants of Levi. Both were of the tribe of Levi and were set apart by God for full-time work at the temple. The priest had the responsibility of offering sacrifices at the temple, presenting incense, and conducting the morning and evening services of the temple. The office of the Levites was to assist the priests in their services. In the journey of the Israelites through the wilderness going from one location to another, it was their duty to transport the various parts of the tabernacle and the sacred utensils. They also saw that the tabernacle and the temple were kept clean, along with preparing supplies for the sanctuary such as oil, incense, and wine, which were used in great quantities.

Because the route being traveled was a long journey, it is possible the Levite could earlier have seen ahead and watched as the priest went around the wounded man. Perhaps he thought, "Well, if he is not going to do anything about it, then I'm not going to either." The Levite refused to take responsibility. Sadly enough, the language used by Jesus strongly implies that the Levite took a thorough look at the wounded man; it was not a fleeting glance.

Once when I was journeying through a rural area of Uganda, we were driving swiftly along a dirt road when suddenly I saw a woman lying in a ditch. I told the driver, "Stop the car!"

The pastor riding along with us cautioned me, "Pastor Steven, please be very careful. If you touch that woman, in our culture it means you take full responsibility for her."

I said, "It's OK, stop anyhow." I got out and walked up to the woman. Upon looking at her I couldn't tell if she were unconscious or dead. One thing I did notice was a gigantic lump on her forehead which she apparently suffered from having just fallen off of a motorcycle. In some countries, the women ride on the back of the motorcycle while being positioned sideways in an effort to appear modest, although it creates a real challenge to properly balance oneself.

Quickly, I laid my hands on her limp body and said, "In the name of Jesus, get up." Instantly, her eyes opened and she sat up and grabbed her head and mumbled some words in the Luganda language which I couldn't understand. At that moment, I heard police sirens coming in the near distance, so I jumped back in the car and we took off just as the police car came over the hill. They stopped next to the woman and began to minister aid. I knew from that point on the woman was in good hands. So I can understand what the priest and Levite were facing; they were required to abide by the regulations of the law. The priest would represent to us the strict moral requirements of the law. The Levite represents the ceremonial aspects of the law. The Apostle Paul tells us that the law was tutor to bring us to Christ, so that we may be justified by faith. The following verse has to be one of the sweetest things you'll ever hear.

For the law was given through Moses, but grace and truth came through Jesus Christ (John 1:17).

The Levite continued on his journey while the beaten man still lay hopelessly in the dirt. The vultures continued to watch, ready to soon start their own specialized work of keeping the desert clean.

But a certain Samaritan, as he journeyed, came where he was. And when he saw him, he had compassion (Luke 10:33).

The Samaritans were a mixed race of people. When the majority of Jews were carried away into Babylonian captivity, the land was left unoccupied except for the poor who were allowed to stay behind. While the Jews were in captivity, the king of Assyria took advantage of the situation and sent people from throughout various regions of his kingdom to inhabit the vacant land of the Jews. These people were heathen idol worshipers who brought their occult practices into the land of Israel. They ran into a real problem when God sent lions and wild beasts throughout the land. Realizing this was a direct consequence of having offended the "God of Israel," they had a Jewish priest sent to them from Babylon to teach them how to honor the God of the Jews. Over time, this produced a people who externally held to certain teachings of Judaism while still primarily embracing the worship of their idols. In essence, the Samaritans created a counterfeit form of Judaism.

Eventually Jews begin to return from Babylon, particularly Nehemiah with the goal of rebuilding the temple. It's interesting when you read how the Samaritans offered to help Nehemiah in the building process, but he strictly refused their help, perceiving their motives and intentions were not genuine toward serving God. The Samaritans then revealed their true jealousy and dislike of the Jewish religion by trying to hinder Nehemiah and the temple builders in many ways, such as shouting constant verbal discouragement and long, drawn-out, complicated law suits. This was the beginning of the strife between the Jews and Samaritans.

The Samaritans went on to build their own temple on Mount Gerizim, which was about 40 miles north of Jerusalem. Sanballat was their leader, and he set his own son into position as the high priest of the temple. The Samaritans boldly declared that it was on this mountain that proper worship was to take place. The ruins from the Samaritan temple still remain till this day. You can see this in the classic Bible story of the Samaritan woman at the well telling Jesus that her ancestors worshiped on Mount Gerizim. Jesus responded by telling her:

Woman, believe Me, the hour is coming when you will neither on this mountain, nor in Jerusalem, worship the Father. You worship what you do not know; we know what we worship, for salvation is of the Jews (John 4:21-22).

Jesus was kind, but He did not mince words. He went on to reveal Himself to this woman as the Messiah, whom she and much of the city gladly received.

Before this, to further irritate the Jews the Samaritans openly proclaimed that their community was open to receiving all Jewish outlaws, Jewish criminals, and any Jew who was a violator of justice. In the year A.D. 6, a group of Samaritans came down to Jerusalem during Passover and defiled the Jerusalem Temple by scattering bones in it. Jewish pilgrims traveling south from Galilee to Jerusalem for the feast days were always afraid of going through Samaritan territory. There are historical records that tell of a whole group of Jewish pilgrims going to one of the feasts in Israel, who were slaughtered while attempting to quietly pass through Samaria. For these antagonizing reasons along with the compilation of many others, the Jews viewed the Samaritans as the lowest class of humans on the face of the earth. Yet, it was the Samaritan who stopped and rendered aid to the wounded Jewish man.

So he went to him and bandaged his wounds, pouring on oil and wine; and he set him on his own animal, brought him to an inn, and took care of him (Luke 10:34).

There are certain people who not only want to be a blessing, but they prepare themselves to be a blessing. This Samaritan actually carried bandages, oil, and wine with him. It would appear as if he had planned for such an event. I would not be the least bit surprised if he had rendered aid to others before who were in similar situations. The buzzards sitting on the rocks watching the wounded man now realized they were going to have to look elsewhere for a meal. The Good Samaritan had made it another bad day for the buzzards.

Fasting keeps the spirit strong and tends to keep the spirit, and give it control over the body. When a person fasts, and brings their body into travail before God, their spirit becomes stronger, and in harmony with God. So I find that in fasting, it gives me greater power to pray with people, or for people's diseases. It gives me greater power with God to preach the word, and the revivals are a greater success. I feel that if a man should ever quit fasting, he is losing out in his ministry and in his life for God. "When you are weak then you are strong." This is a separated life. God showed me at the very beginning of this ministry, that it was a separated life, that I must spend many hours fasting, praying, meditating, and staying before the Lord. —James Dunn

You can also upend the devil's evil intentions toward others by intervening with divine mercy and help. The Good Samaritan is like the modern-day person who carries a trusty pair of jumper cables in his vehicle trunk, just looking for someone whose car battery is dead so they may help recharge it while using it as an avenue to share the Gospel. I have a neighbor who is a retired chief firefighter who always carries a large, multi-gallon container of gasoline in the back of his pickup truck. He constantly comes across people who have their vehicles pulled off on the side of the road because they ran out of gas. He gives them enough gas to safely make it to the nearest gas station. He has helped countless people. These are people with Good Samaritan mind-sets who not only have good intentions, but actually plan out and implement ways in which they can help others in times of need.

> *On the next day, when he departed, he took out two denarii, gave them to the innkeeper, and said to him, "Take care of him; and whatever more you spend, when I come again, I will repay you"* (Luke 10:35).

To be in the position to properly render aid to your "neighbor," you need to be blessed. The Samaritan put the wounded Jewish man on his own animal. In other words, he had a means of transportation, which in our modern day world would be a good vehicle. He drove the man to the hotel and paid for his hotel bill, and then he told the clerk that if more money was owed upon his return he would pay that as well. Back in those days, if you didn't pay your bill you went to jail. This Samaritan had financial reserves so that his needs were met and he had the extra to reach out and bless others in need. God wants you to be like the Good Samaritan and always have a money reserve on hand that is available for those special needs that will certainly come your way.

To embrace the doctrine that it is God's will for you to be poor, is to embrace a lie along with the full functioning of the curse brought into the earth through sin. The Church needs to finally stop romanticizing poverty and recognize it for what it really is. I used to be a homeless person. For months upon months, I ate out of trash cans and dumpsters.[1] If there was anything romantic about poverty, it quickly evaporated after my first day in a cardboard box. Romance should smell good. But I found when I searched through the dumpsters for food, that nothing ever smelled good. Garbage doesn't smell good, hell doesn't smell good, and poverty is directly from hell. I know that sounds shocking, but the church needs to be in a position of overflow—not shortage and lack. Poor people cannot buy bandages for the sick, cannot put someone up in a hotel room, cannot transport someone to a necessary destination, and cannot pay for someone else's bill. To be Good Samaritans, we need to embrace Jehovah Jireh (The Lord Your Provider) and walk in His abundance.

Jesus closed out His amazing story, defining who our neighbor really is.

> *"So which of these three do you think was neighbor to him who fell among the thieves?" And he said, "He who showed mercy on him." Then Jesus said to him, "Go and do likewise"* (Luke 10:36-37).

The Jewish lawyer who initially asked Jesus *"Who is my neighbor?"* replied correctly to Jesus, but notice that he didn't even mention that the person who responded correctly was the Samaritan. This lawyer refused to even use the "dirty" word "Samaritan," only mentioning this man as *"He who showed mercy on him."*

Jesus commanded you and me to *"Go and do likewise."* The world is our "neighbor." We don't get to pick and choose who we find wounded and lying on the road. The steps of a righteous man are ordered of the Lord. As we walk in a state of preparation, opportunities will come on a regular basis. When you fast and pray, the Lord will place within you a new compassion to function in an ongoing way like the Good Samaritan. You will find yourself helping the poor like Job who was a *father to the poor* and *searched out the case that he did not know* (see Job 29:16). A new level of joy will spring into your heart. A new level of authority will be granted to you from on high. Surely you will know with deep conviction that as you consider the poor, the Lord will deliver you in your time of trouble (see Ps. 41:1). The Holy Spirit will highlight these truths to you as you meditate on the greatest chapter on fasting that is recorded in the Bible, Isaiah 58. I want to encourage you to take time to contemplate these truths in this chapter while on your fast, for they will lead you into a richer dimension of God's blessings.

Endnote

1. Steven Brooks, *The Sacred Anointing* (Shippensburg, PA: Destiny Image Publishers, 2010), 35.

CHAPTER TEN

21-DAY FAST DIARY

Introduction

I FELT IT WOULD BE beneficial to share with you a 21-day fast that I recently completed. While fasting I kept a journal and briefly shared some thoughts from each day's experience. This will show you the ups and downs that can be associated with fasting and will offer you an insight into what an extended fast is like.

The day before I started my fast, I drove with Kelly to a local mountain resort town to have a fun day. We made a stop at my favorite sub sandwich shop where we ate, laughed, and enjoyed our time together. We finished up our day at a great coffeehouse where I had a caramel macchiato latte and a large cinnamon roll. Later that night after returning home, I watched some television with Abigail while eating a bag of dried plums. Now my mind is prepared for the fast which I entered into at exactly 8:30 p.m. of this day.

The purpose of this fast is twofold. For the last few years, I have set aside times of prayer and fasting seeking the Lord for an outpouring of His Spirit. The desire to see a genuine revival with notable miracles has been heavy on my heart each time I sought the Lord. After many seasons of prayer, I finally received a promise directly from the Lord while quietly resting a few days ago. The Lord Jesus spoke to my heart, not with a thunderous voice, but with a gentle whisper that I could barely hear. He said, "If you seek Me again, He will come." Instantly I knew the Lord Jesus was referring to the Holy Spirit. Just as the Holy Spirit fell upon the 120 in the Upper Room and empowered them with divine ability, so too have I known that we need a fresh anointing to meet the needs of our spiritually-dark area. So I step into this fast with earnest pleas for the Lord to send the mighty Holy Spirit into our midst.

Secondly, I will be in prayer for God's favor and provision that we might purchase land and build our envisioned television recording studio. The construction of this new facility will be utilized for our primary means of international outreach, which is through television and internet media.

Therefore, the two goals of the fast are clearly set before me and I can focus my prayers directly toward these Holy Spirit-led projects which I believe are the will of God.

Day One

My day started rather normal. Before going to the office I had some good time in prayer. Around lunchtime I had to drop my daughter off at art class. Kelly decided to buy a Pizza at Domino's so my daughter could share it with the teacher and students at art. Of course it somehow ends up that I'm holding the pizza box in the car while Kelly drives. I must admit that smelling that pizza made me think about resetting my start date for my fast. But I somehow made it through this. Pizza has always been my favorite food. I finished the day drinking mainly water and some green-looking juice that looked strange but tasted good.

Day Two

This was a classic "doozy" day with constant mild headaches and an overall "blah" feeling. I have no doubt the headaches are primarily related to my withdrawal symptoms of not drinking caffeinated coffee. My tongue has been completely coated with white toxic discharge, and feelings of nausea have been off and on. My energy level has been somewhat low but I did take a nice, slow walk of about one mile to enjoy the sunshine. The Lord has strengthened me, and I have had very strong times of prayer which I believe have been very effective. I drank primarily juice today, a little over half a gallon of grape juice.

Day Three

Having now completed three days of this fast, I can say I feel I am off to a good start. The headaches due to detoxification have been very mild today, and my energy level has been good. I took a nap during the afternoon for about 20 minutes, which helped. We had a great prayer meeting during our noontime corporate prayer at church. It's so easy to pray when fasting; the prayers just seem to flow out. My hunger for food is still slightly hanging around, although not too much of a pull. I must admit I have had a few flashbacks to that pepperoni pizza that I passed up on Day One of my fast. That sure would be good now with a large Coca-Cola.

Day Four

I felt pretty sluggish today, so upon awakening I read my Bible for an hour and spent some time after that in prayer.

Once I was up and moving for the day I felt OK and ended up accomplishing a lot of things that needed to get done at the office. In the evening I found myself low on energy so I went to bed early. I would have liked to spend more time in prayer but the Lord understands. Hopefully tomorrow I can find more time for prayer.

Day Five

Off to a good start with some good morning prayer time accomplished. I was also able to complete a lot of ministry work throughout the day. I worked from 9:00 a.m. until 10:30 p.m. and then took a 30-minute break. I started praying at 11:00 p.m. and didn't stop until 4:00 a.m. I felt like I was a fireman's water hose that got hooked up to a water hydrant and opened to maximum flow. The Holy Spirit was a tremendous helper as I prayed fervently in tongues and in English. My vocal chords are pretty tired from having prayed so long, but in my heart I sense much was accomplished. The Holy Spirit seemed to highlight specific areas to focus on in prayer with laser-like precision.

Day Six

Years ago when I was able to go deep-sea fishing, I remember what it was like when you venture out into deep waters and leave land far behind. There is a point when all you see is water in all directions, having gone beyond the sight of land. When venturing out into the Gulf of Mexico, you eventually pass beyond the continental shelf and the water turns a different shade of color from light blue to dark blue. From this point forward, the water is very deep and the potential to catch big fish is now at hand.

This is the way I feel now in my spirit on this fast. The hunger for food has lifted, and I can focus clearly on prayer without being distracted. This evening at church we had our corporate prayer meeting. All the saints who came prayed with great passion and we were of one heart. My voice was still tired from the previous day, so I had to be careful not to strain it. There continues to be a thickly-coated white residue of toxic discharge on my tongue, so I have been mindful to brush my teeth often and scrub my tongue in the process. Overall it has been another blessed day and I sense the Lord's presence in a clear way.

Day Seven

Today I crossed the timeline of having fasted with no food for seven full days. It feels satisfying knowing a full week has been accomplished. Each day I am drinking almost one gallon of water and about 48 ounces of apple juice.

Day Eight

No spiritual fireworks today, everything was just as normal as could be. I weighed myself and saw that I have lost eight pounds, which would be a pound per day. I read my Bible in the evening but nothing particular seemed to leap out and grab me. Last night I experienced some discomfort in my legs when trying to sleep. I'm not sure what's causing it; it feels like mini cramps. I'll try some light stretching and see if that helps.

Day Nine

Today was a good day of prayer. My energy level is pretty low so I drank extra juice to give myself a boost. By noon I was feeling better and ended up completing a lot of work that needed to get finished. I went to bed early at 8 p.m. after reading my Bible for an hour.

Day Ten

I had very good times of prayer today during the morning, noon, and then at night before going to bed. The sun was shining today; I always like it when the weather is nice. The warm sunshine feels so good on my face, especially since I get cold easily when fasting. The apple juice seems to be getting somewhat boring. Tomorrow I may try a different type of juice. The leg cramps from the previous day have thankfully disappeared.

Day Eleven

I took a nice walk today of about one mile. Time seems to definitely be slowing down. The day seems to last a long time. Today I prayed for what I thought was 2 hours, but when I looked at my watch only 20 minutes had gone by. There's definitely no need to rush; I'll just keep taking this one day at a time.

Day Twelve

I can "feel" the effects of the time I have spent lately meditating on God's Word. On the inside (in my spirit) it just seems so easy to believe that there is nothing that God can't do. If some type of amazing miracle were to happen in front of me right now I don't think I would be the least bit surprised. In my present state, a miracle would appear to be a normal event. Reading God's Word coupled with the fasting and extra time in prayer seems to have sent my faith through the roof.

Day Thirteen

I woke up this morning feeling great but as the day progressed my patience was tested. Small things like the sound of paper being crumpled, or potato chips being loudly crunched by someone as they eat seem to bring forth an unusual irritation within me. I know this edginess is simply due to my fasting which causes all of my senses to be heightened. Normally these things wouldn't bother me. This is an indicator that I need to continue in prayer to remain in the Spirit.

Day Fourteen

It feels comforting knowing that another week is accomplished and that only one week remains. Today I spent time in prayer, but also spent much time reading my Bible as I was greatly blessed by reading the complete Gospel of Matthew. I weighed myself and have lost 12 pounds since I started.

One morning when I came down to breakfast, I found my appetite had disappeared. I could not eat. I went about my work as usual. At dinner I had no desire to eat, and no more in the evening. This went on till the third day. But toward the evening of the third day, an overwhelming desire to pray took possession of me. I wanted only to be

181

alone to pray. Prayer flowed from my soul like a stream. I could not cease praying. As soon as it was possible to get to a place of seclusion, I would kneel to pour out my heart to God for hours. Whatever I was doing, that stream of prayer continued flowing from my soul. On the night of the sixth day of this fast, that the Lord had laid on me, while in the act of washing my hands, the Spirit said, "How long have you been praying to cast out demons?" and I replied, "Lord, a long time." And the Spirit said, "From henceforth, thou shalt cast out demons." I arose and praised God. —John G. Lake

(An opportunity to test this newly-given anointing to cast out demons came the following Sunday, when a violently insane man was brought to Lake, who commanded the demon to come out of him in Jesus' name. The man was instantly delivered, and two days later was released from the institution that he had been confined in.)

Day Fifteen

We had a very sweet day at church. The service flowed smoothly and the Spirit's power was manifested with wonderful healings. Physically, I can tell my strength is low but spiritually speaking there is a keen awareness in my heart to the direction that the Spirit wished to take in the service. I feel like a horse whose reins need only be gently touched by the rider (the Holy

Spirit), being able to almost read the mind of the rider and instantly respond.

Day Sixteen

Today was a good day to rest and meditate upon God's promises which I am standing on. I felt impressed to spend extra time thanking and praising God for all He has done, as well as praising Him for the unseen things He is doing which I believe by faith He is bringing to pass.

Day Seventeen

Today proved to be very discouraging. It seemed as if the heavens were brass. Even my most earnest prayers felt ineffective and futile. I also found myself grumpy and very short-tempered, so it was best that I was not around anyone while at the church office. It was as if weights of discouragement were heaped upon my soul. Questions flooded my mind such as, "Will God really answer my prayers?" I tried reading my Bible, even changing positions, eventually going for a walk, but nothing seemed to change the feelings of hopelessness. Every time I would try to read something from the Psalms it seemed as if all I saw were verses such as the following;

Have mercy on me, O Lord, for I am in trouble; ...My eye wastes away with grief, yes, my soul and my body! For my life is spent with grief, and my years with sighing; my strength fails because of my iniquity, and my bones waste away. I am a reproach among all my enemies, but especially among my neighbors, and am repulsive to my acquaintances; those who see me outside flee from me. I am forgotten like a dead man, out of mind; I am like a broken vessel. For I hear the slander of many; fear is on every side; while they take counsel together against me, they scheme to take away my life (Psalms 31:9-13).

Toward the end of the day, I began to refocus and realize that I must choose to walk by faith and not judge things by the way I felt emotionally. This day felt like God was millions of miles away, but I ended the day by telling the Lord, "Despite my mood of feeling forsaken, I trust Your Word, and I believe You will make a way for me." That night I went to bed under a heavy burden of despondency.

Day Eighteen

When I woke up this morning and sat up in bed, it seemed as if golden rays of light were flooding into my soul. Talk about doing a complete 180-degree turn; the difference from the day before could only be described like the contrast of night and day. Every Scripture that I looked at today seemed to be bursting with divine life. My prayer time was so anointed it seemed as if God were sitting on the couch next to me. The spiritual reality of Isaiah 58:10 hit me with full force.

…Then your light shall dawn in the darkness, and your darkness shall be as the noonday (Isaiah 58:10).

The Lord quickened my spirit as I reread through some of the same psalms that I went over the day before. Now I had a much better understanding of David's grief and sorrow which he expressed in his writings. David openly revealed his deepest feelings so that we could identify with the same spiritual journey as we progress in our walk with the Lord. *"Weeping may endure for a night, but joy comes in the morning"* (Ps. 30:5). A great calm now rests upon my soul; I sense in my heart that my voice *is* being heard on high.

Surely I have calmed and quieted my soul, like a weaned child with his mother; like a weaned child is my soul within me (Psalms 131:2).

Day Nineteen

Early in the morning, I awoke from a horrible dream sent by the enemy. The dream was of a mass murderer (the devil), and he was angry with me and threatening to kill me. Hordes of demons surrounded me and were attempting to attack me, but they could not press through an invisible shield around me. The dream conveyed much fear and anger from the adversary. When I awoke I saw that it was 4:00 a.m., and I could feel the lingering negative effects of the dream. These nightmares come as a form of spiritual attack, but their horrific images quickly dissolve away when confronted by the Lord's true authority. On purpose, I got up and went into prayer for one solid hour, asking God for His anointing to increase upon me that He might continue to heal the sick through me with mighty demonstrations of the Spirit's power. After prayer, my heart was filled with peace and I then went back to sleep for a few hours before rising to pray again.

And the God of peace will crush Satan under your feet shortly... (Romans 16:20).

Day Twenty

This morning I awoke at 5:00 a.m. and entered into prayer until 8:00 a.m. Following prayer time, I then read my Bible for another 30 minutes before getting ready for the day and going down to the church to do my necessary work. I can feel that I am on the home stretch, but I am not letting up on my prayer time. Pleasing thoughts about being able to eat food again are fun to think about, but until I cross the finish line I am staying fully focused on my prayer assignments.

It seems the Holy Spirit is emphasizing today the ministry of the angels. I sense in my heart that knotty problems are being dissolved and worked out by the Lord's strong angels. This evening we had a church service. During the service, an unmistakable smell of sweet flowers permeated the meeting place, which about 90 percent of the congregation smelled. There were no natural flowers in the building, and the fragrance would swirl around, sometimes being gentle and other times increasing in intensity.

I shared with the people that they would be anointed with the fresh oil of the Spirit and that some of them would go into visions. One of the testimonies received afterward was of a young girl of 11 years of age who went into a vision when I anointed her forehead with anointing oil. She said Jesus was standing in our midst surrounded by beautiful flowers. She could clearly see His nailed-pierced hands as His blood was dripping from His hands onto white flowers. The sweet heavenly fragrance of flowers continued throughout the entire service.

One lady who was a guest visitor from out of state came and testified of how she was completely healed from multiple sclerosis. She said that I prayed for her last year during the healing service in Jerusalem while on our tour of Israel. I remember distinctly laying my hands on her during that service and telling her that she was healed of her disease. Upon returning home she went back to her doctor for a checkup, and the doctor informed her that there was no longer any multiple sclerosis anywhere in her body. That was almost a year ago and she has been healed ever since. Praise God for His healing power.

Day Twenty-One

This is my last day of the fast and tomorrow I can enjoy the pleasure of eating. During this fast I have lost 17 pounds. Tomorrow is the biblical Feast of Pentecost (Shavuot), so there will be an abundance of food. However, I won't be able to eat much because my stomach has shrunk due to not eating for 21 days. So I will start with a small meal and work my way up over the next few days. I will continue to keep pressing in, but I have a calm assurance that God has heard my prayers over the last three weeks, and now I look forward with expectancy in the ways in which He will surely answer.

Conclusion

As we close, I would like to leave you with the thought that as you fast and pray the power of God will surely be made available to you. You have the potential before you to make tremendous strides forward in your walk with the Lord. God is waiting for you to draw near. Will you go and meet Him in the secret place? The secret place has always been a place of fasting and prayer. I encourage you today to take your place among the great saints of past history who responded to the call of "deep unto deep." God is calling you now to fast and pray that your spiritual eyes may be opened in a greater measure.

You are that person God wants to work through to do mighty works. The greatest power known to man in the physical world is nuclear power. Allow God to fill you with His heavenly nuclear power. God is calling you to become radioactive with His love, His glory, His faith, and His compassion. As you fast and pray you will be overshadowed with the glory of God. Just as the cherubim spread their wings and covered the mercy seat over the Ark of the Covenant, so too will you be enshrouded in the Lord's presence. May the Lord bless you as you seek His face with all of your heart through fasting and prayer.

Prayer and Fasting Commitment

This short form is given here as a mental reminder of why you are fasting and also to serve as a record of the number of days in which you will fast. It will prove useful in helping you to fulfill your fast by putting in writing your intentions and expectations. Often when we put something in writing and add our signature to it we feel more "locked in" and committed to our goal.

Purpose of the Fast:

_____

Type of Fast (water, juice, etc.):

_____

Intended Duration of the Fast:

_____

Begin Date: _____

Begin Time: _____

End Date: _____

End Time: _____

Verbal Commitment: Heavenly Father, in the Name of Jesus, I commit to fast for _____ (amount of time), for the specific purpose of seeing You accomplish _____. Knowing that nothing is impossible with You, I enter this designated fast with faith and expectancy that You will hear my prayers, regard my fasting, and thus reward me openly. May the glory be Yours. In Jesus' Name I pray, amen.

The following Scriptures are the support and basis for my purpose of fasting:

1. _____

2. _____

3. _____

Signed: _____

Date: _____

PRAYER OF SALVATION AND TO BE FILLED WITH THE HOLY SPIRIT AND FIRE

Perhaps you came across this book and have not yet had the opportunity to personally receive Jesus Christ as Savior and Lord. I would like to invite you to open your heart to Him now. Please read the following verses from the Bible out loud. When you read Bible verses out loud, it allows bold faith to enter into your heart.

And it shall come to pass that whoever calls on the name of the Lord shall be saved (Acts 2:21).

That if you confess with your mouth the Lord Jesus and believe in your heart that God has raised Him from the dead, you will be saved (Romans 10:9).

And do not be drunk with wine, in which is dissipation [debauchery]; but be filled with the Spirit (Ephesians 5:18).

And they were all filled with the Holy Spirit and began to speak with other tongues, as the Spirit gave them utterance (Acts 2:4).

Now that you have read how you may be saved, you can obey the Word of God and make your life right with God. Simply pray the following prayer from your heart and Jesus will give you His eternal life.

Dear Lord Jesus, today I choose to make You my Lord and Savior. I confess that You are the Son of God. I believe that You were raised from the dead and are alive forevermore. Please come into my heart and forgive me of all my sins. I turn away from all sin and I give my life completely to You. Please fill me with Your precious Holy Spirit so that I may speak in tongues and worship You all the days of my life. I receive Your salvation now, and I praise You for it. Thank You, Jesus, for saving me and for filling me with Your Holy Spirit.

Now lift your hands and begin to praise God for saving you. Open your mouth and begin to speak in the new heavenly language that the Holy Spirit has given you. Let the new words and syllables come forth—not your own language, but the language the Holy Spirit gives you. Don't be concerned about how it sounds. It might not make sense to your mind, but it is your spirit communicating with God, and God understands everything you are speaking.

Praise the Lord! You are now a Spirit-filled Christian on your way to Heaven. Every day speak in tongues to glorify God and to strengthen yourself. You will be refreshed as you do.

Now that you belong to Jesus, ask your Heavenly Father to help you find a new church home so that you can grow spiritually and continue your walk with God. The Holy Spirit will lead you as you search for the Christian church that God wants you to be a part of. Look for a church where you can sense the love of God and where people take a genuine interest in your spiritual growth. Seek out a church that believes the whole Bible and preaches it without compromise. And always remember that *God loves you.*

Additional Scripture
on Prayer and Fasting

Years ago, I worked the night shift of a security job at an exclusive gated community, which due to its slow pace offered me the opportunity to pray hours at a time. I would start work at 7:00 p.m. and finish at 3:30 a.m. After 11:00 p.m., the whole community was as quiet as a mouse. I could then pray for an hour, jump on my golf cart and make a round through the property, and then continue in prayer for another hour before repeating the process till my shift ended. Once, after concluding a time of prayer, I stood up from my kneeling position and felt an unusual breeze blowing against my knees. Reaching down to my knees and feeling around, I discovered that I had worn large holes through each leg of my black jeans in the knee area. The jeans were black and thick so I hadn't noticed this before, since when standing up the gap would appear not to be there, unless flexed. I now had to purchase a new pair of jeans for work. The holes in the jeans were created from me praying in a kneeling position for hours on end. I guess those could be called "holy" jeans. Today, I am convinced one of the primary reasons God has blessed me with a global miracle ministry is because of the foundation of prayer that was laid in my life years before I went into full-time ministry.

In this Appendix I have listed some additional Scriptures about the great value of prayer, fasting, and not overeating. Faith comes by hearing, so I believe these selected Scriptures will inspire faith in you to develop a strong spiritual foundation in your life by following these biblical principles.

Then I proclaimed a fast there at the river of Ahava, that we might humble ourselves before our God, to seek from Him the right way for us and our little ones and all our possessions (Ezra 8:21).

So we fasted and entreated our God for this, and He answered our prayer (Ezra 8:23).

And in every province where the king's command and decree arrived, there was great mourning among the Jews, with fasting, weeping, and wailing; and many lay in sackcloth and ashes (Esther 4:3).

Go, gather all the Jews who are present in Shushan, and fast for me; neither eat nor drink for three days, night or day. My maids and I will fast likewise. And so I will go to the king, which is against the law; and if I perish, I perish! (Esther 4:16)

Is this not the fast that I have chosen: to loose the bonds of wickedness, to undo the heavy burdens, to let the oppressed go free, and that you break every yoke? Is it not to share your bread with the hungry, and that you bring to your house the poor who are cast out; when you see the naked, that you cover him, and not hide yourself from your own flesh? Then your light shall break forth like the morning, your healing shall spring forth speedily, and your righteousness shall go before you; the glory of the Lord shall be your rear guard. Then you shall call, and the Lord will answer; you shall cry, and He will say, "Here I am."

If you take away the yoke from your midst, the pointing of the finger, and speaking wickedness, if you extend your soul to the hungry and satisfy the afflicted soul, then your light shall dawn in the darkness, and your darkness shall be as the noonday. The Lord will guide you continually, and satisfy your soul in drought, and strengthen your bones; you shall be like a watered garden, and like a spring of water, whose waters do not fail. Those from among you shall build the old waste places; you shall raise up the foundations of many generations; and you shall be called the Repairer of the Breach, The Restorer of Streets to Dwell In (Isaiah 58:6-12).

Then all the children of Israel, that is, all the people, went up and came to the house of God and wept. They sat there before the Lord and fasted that day until evening; and they offered burnt offerings and peace offerings before the Lord (Judges 20:26).

So they gathered together at Mizpah, drew water, and poured it out before the Lord. And they fasted that day, and said there, "We have sinned against the Lord." And Samuel judged the children of Israel at Mizpah (1 Samuel 7:6).

And they mourned and wept and fasted until evening for Saul and for Jonathan his son, for the people of the Lord and for the house of Israel, because they had fallen by the sword (2 Samuel 1:12).

So it was, when Ahab heard those words, that he tore his clothes and put sackcloth on his body, and fasted and lay in sackcloth, and went about mourning (1 Kings 21:27).

Say to all the people of the land, and to the priests: "When you fasted and mourned in the fifth and seventh months during those seventy years, did you really fast for Me—for Me?" (Zechariah 7:5)

At the evening sacrifice I arose from my fasting; and having torn my garment and my robe, I fell on my knees and spread out my hands to the Lord my God (Ezra 9:5).

So it was, when I heard these words, that I sat down and wept, and mourned for many days; I was fasting and praying before the God of heaven (Nehemiah 1:4).

Now on the twenty-fourth day of this month the children of Israel were assembled with fasting, in sackcloth, and with dust on their heads (Nehemiah 9:1).

But as for me, when they were sick, my clothing was sackcloth; I humbled myself with fasting; and my prayer would return to my own heart (Psalms 35:13).

My knees are weak through fasting, and my flesh is feeble from lack of fatness (Psalms 109:24).

Now the king went to his palace and spent the night fasting; and no musicians were brought before him. Also his sleep went from him (Daniel 6:18).

Then I set my face toward the Lord God to make request by prayer and supplications, with fasting, sackcloth, and ashes (Daniel 9:3).

"Now, therefore," says the Lord, "Turn to Me with all your heart, with fasting, with weeping, and with mourning" (Joel 2:12).

Moreover, when you fast, do not be like the hypocrites, with a sad countenance. For they disfigure their faces that they may appear to men to be fasting. Assuredly, I say to you, they have their reward. But you, when you fast, anoint your head and wash your face, so that you do not appear to men to be fasting, but to your Father who is in the secret place; and your Father who sees in secret will reward you openly (Matthew 6:16-18).

However, this kind does not go out except by prayer and fasting (Matthew 17:21).

So He said to them, "This kind can come out by nothing but prayer and fasting" (Mark 9:29).

So Cornelius said, "Four days ago I was fasting until this hour; and at the ninth hour I prayed in my house, and behold, a man stood before me in bright clothing" (Acts 10:30).

As they ministered to the Lord and fasted, the Holy Spirit said, "Now separate to Me Barnabas and Saul for the work to which I have called them." Then, having fasted and prayed, and laid hands on them, they sent them away (Acts 13:2-3).

So when they had appointed elders in every church, and prayed with fasting, they commended them to the Lord in whom they had believed (Acts 14:23).

Do not deprive one another except with consent for a time, that you may give yourselves to fasting and prayer; and come together again so that Satan does not tempt you because of your lack of self-control (1 Corinthians 7:5).

And when He had fasted forty days and forty nights, afterward He was hungry (Matthew 4:2).

Then Jesus, again groaning in Himself, came to the tomb. It was a cave, and a stone lay against it (John 11:38).

For we know that the whole creation groans and labors with birth pangs together until now. Not only that, but we also who have the firstfruits of the Spirit, even we ourselves groan within ourselves, eagerly waiting for the adoption, the redemption of our body (Romans 8:22-23).

Who, in the days of His flesh, when He had offered up prayers and supplications, with vehement cries and tears to Him who was able to save Him from death, and was heard because of His godly fear (Hebrews 5:7).

Likewise the Spirit also helps in our weaknesses. For we do not know what we should pray for as we ought, but the Spirit Himself makes intercession for us with groanings which cannot be uttered. Now He who searches the hearts knows what the mind of the Spirit is, because He makes intercession for the saints according to the will of God (Romans 8:26-27).

...For as soon as Zion was in labor, she gave birth to her children (Isaiah 66:8).

So I sought for a man among them who would make a wall, and stand in the gap before Me on behalf of the land, that I should not destroy it; but I found no one (Ezekiel 22:30).

...He will come to us like the rain, like the latter and former rain to the earth (Hosea 6:3).

Ask the Lord for rain in the time of the latter rain... (Zechariah 10:1).

Let the priests, who minister to the Lord, weep between the porch and the altar; let them say, "Spare Your people, O Lord, and do not give Your heritage to reproach, that the nations should rule over them. Why should they say among the peoples, 'Where is their God?'" (Joel 2:17)

He saw that there was no man, and wondered that there was no intercessor; therefore His own arm brought salvation for Him; and His own righteousness, it sustained Him (Isaiah 59:16).

MINISTRY PARTNER INFORMATION

We would like to share with you a sincere and open invitation to partner with the life-changing ministry of Steven Brooks International. With the support of our precious ministry partners, Pastor Steven and Kelly are empowered to reach further into the nations of the world with God's Word and His healing touch. Working together, we can experience a greater impact for the fulfillment of the Great Commission. With a world population approaching the staggering number of seven billion souls, the need has never been greater for anointed biblical teaching coupled with genuine manifestations of God's power to strengthen the Church.

Pastor Steven's life is dedicated toward the apostolic cause of ministering the bread of life to hungry souls around the world. Without the help of dedicated ministry partners, the great outreaches of this ministry would not be possible. The help of each ministry partner is vital. Whether the support is large or if it is the widow's last two pennies, every bit helps in this worldwide outreach. With your prayers and generous financial support, we are continuing to go through the unprecedented doors of opportunity which the Lord is opening for this ministry.

Pastor Steven and Kelly absolutely treasure their ministry partners. Each ministry partner is viewed as a special gift from God and is to be highly valued. Pastor Steven and Kelly believe in covenant relationships and understand the emphasis and blessing that God places upon such divine connections. In this end-time hour, God is joining those with like hearts to stand together in this sacred work. Thank you for prayerfully considering becoming a ministry partner. We encourage you to take the step and join this exciting and rewarding journey with us. Together we can make an eternal difference in the lives of precious souls, enabling us to have an expectancy to hear the Lord's voice on that blessed day, saying, "Well done, thou good and faithful servant."

As a ministry partner, your undertaking is to pray for Pastor Steven, his family, and his ministry on a regular basis and support his ministry with a monthly financial contribution.

As a ministry partner, you will receive the following benefits:

- Impartation that is upon Pastor Steven's life to be upon you to help you accomplish what God has called you to do

- Consistent prayer for you by Pastor Steven

- Monthly ministry partner newsletter to build your faith and feed your spirit

- Mutual faith in God for His best return on all your giving

- Eternal share in the heavenly rewards obtained through this ministry

Become a ministry partner now!

Name:

Address:

Phone Number:

Email Address:

_____ Yes, Pastor Steven. I join with you in ministry partnership and I (we) stand with you as you continue to preach the Gospel to all the earth and usher in the return of the Lord Jesus Christ.

Please mail your information to:
Steven Brooks International
PO Box 717
Moravian Falls, NC 28654

You may also become a ministry partner by registering at our online Web site at www.stevenbrooks.org.

Click on the "Partner" link to sign up.

For booking information and upcoming meetings regarding Steven Brooks International please visit our website at www.stevenbrooks.org or e-mail us at info@stvenbrooks.org.

For service times and more information about The Holy Place Worship Center, please visit us online at www.theholyplacewc.org.

ABOUT STEVEN BROOKS

The ministry of Steven and Kelly Brooks continues to reach multitudes of souls around the world. Steven is widely known for his ability to teach God's Word in a clear and understandable way to new believers as well as to those who have been in the faith for decades. He walks in a remarkable gift of *working miracles,* and *divine healing* is a trademark of his ministry. Steven stresses the importance of faith in God and the eternal value of living a life of prayer and holiness. His heart is to see the lost saved and the Church strengthened.

Brother Steven stands by grace in the ministry office of the modern-day apostle. As a *sent one,* he is constantly traveling far and wide throughout America and to the most remote areas of the world, preaching the good news of Jesus Christ. Whether in the Himalayan Mountain region or along the Nile River in Africa, Brother Steven has a mandate from God to, *"Go, and teach all nations."* The television show *Fire and Glory* is rapidly growing, with Steven's program now airing in over 45 nations and reaching a potential viewing audience of two billion people. His pulpit messages are streamed live on the internet from The Holy Place Worship Center and are viewed weekly in over 70 nations, including a remarkably large following of viewers in the Asian and European countries.

He is a prolific writer with his books being available in bookstores nationwide, as well as them being translated into different languages and widely distributed overseas.

Steven is senior pastor and co-founder along with his wife Kelly of The Holy Place Worship Center in Moravian Falls, North Carolina. This thriving and dynamic church is considered a hub of revival and healing power. Guests from other countries frequently visit and the sick travel for miles to attend in anticipation of receiving God's healing power. The church is known for its strong prayer foundations and for an atmosphere of love and humility.

In the right hands, This Book will Change Lives!

Most of the people who need this message will not be looking for this book. To change their lives, you need to put a copy of this book in their hands.

> *But others (seeds) fell into good ground, and brought forth fruit, some a hundred-fold, some sixty-fold, some thirty-fold* (Matthew 13:8).

Our ministry is constantly seeking methods to find the good ground, the people who need this anointed message to change their lives. Will you help us reach these people?

> *Remember this—a farmer who plants only a few seeds will get a small crop. But the one who plants generously will get a generous crop* (2 Corinthians 9:6).

EXTEND THIS MINISTRY BY SOWING
3 BOOKS, 5 BOOKS, 10 BOOKS, OR MORE TODAY,
AND BECOME A LIFE CHANGER!

Thank you,

Don Nori Sr., Founder
Destiny Image
Since 1982

DESTINY IMAGE PUBLISHERS, INC.

"Promoting Inspired Lives."

VISIT OUR NEW SITE HOME AT
WWW.DESTINYIMAGE.COM

FREE SUBSCRIPTION TO DI NEWSLETTER

Receive free unpublished articles by top DI authors, exclusive

discounts, and free downloads from our best and newest books.

Visit www.destinyimage.com to subscribe.

Write to: Destiny Image
              P.O. Box 310
              Shippensburg, PA 17257-0310

Call: 1-800-722-6774

Email: orders@destinyimage.com

For a complete list of our titles or to place an order
online, visit www.destinyimage.com.